RICH KID KILLERS OF BEVERLY HILLS

Ronald E Bowers

Former Senior Prosecutor

Los Angeles County District Attorney's Office

Some names and locations have been changed to protect the privacy of individuals connected with these cases. Certain events and statements have been inferred from the facts of these cases as well as from public articles about these cases.

Ronald E. Bowers, Publisher
losangelestruecrime@aol.com

ISBN 978-1-7325281-3-0

First release December 2014
Second release April 2017

INTRODUCTION

True Crime books come to you, the reader, from various sources. I'm sure there will be readers who look at this book and say to themselves that they know all the facts about Joe Hunt, the founder of the Billionaire Boys Club. Many people also know about the protracted jury trials of the Menendez Brothers, who killed their parents. Many readers' initial reaction may be, why revisit old news? A myriad of books and TV movies have explored these cases. However, they were written and produced by outsiders who had limited knowledge of the true stories behind each of those cases. This book provides you, the reader, with a new perspective of looking from the inside out. These two cases have forever been linked together, although the media never focused on the connection. For years I wondered why no one pieced together these sensational cases and revealed all the intrigue that went on behind the scenes for more than a decade.

Since my retirement from the Los Angeles District Attorney's Office, I have had the time to write several authentic True Crime books covering my 43 years of experience actually working on so many legendary cases. The Joe Hunt case, and later the Menendez Brothers case, happened to be two cases I was deeply involved in.

This INTRODUCTION is to give you some understanding of the personal insight that I have about these two amazing cases. The Joe Hunt case occurred during 'my watch' when I was the DA administrator in charge of the DA's offices in South L.A. County. Several years later, the Menendez case unexpectedly came to my attention when the lead prosecutor, David Conn, came to me and asked for my expertise. Over the next few pages, I will describe my role in both cases and provide you a firsthand account of what really happened in those two remarkable cases.

Back in November of 1986, my office in the DA's Office was on the 18th floor of the Criminal Courts Building, which had a marvelous view of the imposing San Gabriel Mountains. On a clear day, I could gaze to the east and see Mt. Baldy with its glistening white snow reaching up to the puffy-clouded sky. Around 3:00 in the afternoon on a Friday, I heard my phone ring at my secretary's station. I was cleaning up my cluttered desk, which was littered with notes and return-phone-call messages from a chaotic week. My job at the time was supervising the operation of the DA's Office in South L.A. County, which consisted of almost 300 attorneys.

I could overhear my secretary transferring a call to me from the personal secretary of the District Attorney, Ira Reiner. I surmised this wasn't a good sign, and I braced myself for what I was about to hear. My secretary said to me, "Mr. Bowers, the DA wants to talk to you regarding the 'Joe Hunt' case."

My scope of responsibility included five branch offices, one of which was the Santa Monica Branch. That office alone had several thousand felony cases pending. Obviously, there was no way I could be familiar with all of the felony cases; however, I was aware of the "Joe Hunt" case, which we called the "Billionaire Boys Club" case. But I thought to myself, why was the DA calling me about the case on Friday afternoon and the case hadn't even started trial yet? As the call was connected to my phone, I could hear the DA's secretary say she would connect me to the DA. She said he was on another call, but as soon as he was finished, she would transfer Mr. Reiner to my line. As I waited, I tried to recollect if there was some new development in the case that I hadn't let the front office know about.

The one cardinal rule that had been engrained in all of the administrators was to immediately brief the front office on all publicity cases. We had all learned the DA didn't want to learn about a new development in a publicity case ***from a reporter***. I couldn't remember any new issues in the Joe Hunt case. As I waited on the line, I reviewed in my mind just what questions still remained outstanding in this case. I knew I had better be able to intelligently talk about this case. After several minutes, I could hear the infamous baritone voice of the DA. Without any pleasantries, such as "How are you doing?" he directly asked me for an update on the Joe Hunt case. I didn't know how much detail he wanted or what his actual concern was. I indicated that Fred Wapner, the lead prosecutor on the case, had left a message saying they were about to start jury selection next week.

That apparently wasn't the answer the boss was looking for. He said, "No no, I mean the TV cameras in the courtroom." At that moment I realized the delicate, bumpy road we were about to go down. Our case totally depended on the cooperation of our key witness, Dean Kelly (pseudonym), who we had in a Witness Protection Program. The judge was considering the request of the TV media to grant full TV coverage of the entire trial. If the TV cameras were to cover the star witness's testimony, it could cause the witness to be in fear for his life. The last thing any witness wanted was for his face to appear on millions of TV sets all across the country.

I started to explain to the DA that live TV coverage could be devastating to the case. I went on to explain the reasons we didn't want cameras in the courtroom. There was complete silence on the other end of the line. After mentioning the potential problem, the DA reminded me the DA's Office policy was to cooperate with the news media. He also made it clear he was concerned that we were not being transparent enough for the media. I started to realize I was on the losing side of this discussion. The DA reiterated his policy of cooperating with the TV news and press reporters. My mind flashed back to several years earlier when I first met the DA shortly after his election. He said, very honestly and directly, that he was a '**Politician.'** This was a new approach for the DA's Office since the previous District Attorneys had been **'prosecutors'** who had come up through the ranks and didn't think of themselves as politicians but as senior prosecutors.

I could see that nothing I said was going to satisfy the DA so I swiftly tried to think of a 'Plan B' to prevent him from giving me an order to tell the prosecutor in the Joe Hunt case he couldn't object to full TV coverage. Whenever there are major issues that can't be resolved easily, the solution in the DA's Office is to schedule a meeting and bring all the interested parties to the table. So my response to the boss was, let me set up a meeting and I would have the litigation prosecutors come downtown and explain their concerns to him.

I could sense a degree of frustration from the DA in that I was not agreeing with him as he would have liked. As powerful as the DA's position was, he recognized he needed to know more of the facts before he made an ultimatum that could be very unpopular with the rank and file attorneys. He asked if everyone could be available on Monday afternoon for such a meeting. He reviewed his calendar and said he had a cancellation at 2:30 p. m., so that would work for him. I agreed to the meeting as well as I offered to contact all the people from the Santa Monica office and have them in his office on Monday at 2:30 p.m.

As soon as I hung up with the DA, I dialed the number for the Head Deputy in the Santa Monica Branch and told him I needed everyone on the Hunt case in the DA's Office on Monday at 2:30 p.m. I sold him on the idea by saying that the DA wanted to hear any objections to the TV coverage on the Hunt case. Within an hour, everyone had been notified, including Fred Wapner and as his colleagues. Everyone was on track for the meeting.

On Monday, November 24, 1986, just three days before Thanksgiving, I had everyone assembled in the District Attorney's Office. I worked out the seating arrangements in the boss's office. I escorted Fred Wapner, the lead prosecutor, to sit in the front and center. After everyone was properly seated, I asked all the prosecutors to introduce themselves to the District Attorney and explain their roles in the case. In order to get off to a good start, I explained to the DA it might be best to have Fred Wapner clarify where the court was with having cameras in the courtroom. My thought was, it would be best to start with the trial attorney voicing his concerns.

Apparently I was wrong. The DA wanted everyone in the room to understand the importance of the news media having access to the actual trial in a case. It began to sound like a civics lecture. The DA emphasized that the public had a right to know what was going on in their courtrooms. "Transparency" was the new buzzword being tossed around to describe what we, as prosecutors, should be more vigilant in protecting.

I could see the surprised expression on Fred's face and the female co-prosecutor in the case. Neither one of them was trying to interfere with the news media's access to the trial. However, they had some legitimate concerns for opposing full TV coverage of the entire trial. I knew the DA liked to pontificate his views and he generally won the discussions by the mere fact few would be willing to stand up to him. His distinguished gray hair and distinctive voice made him an imposing figure, and the TV media loved having his 'sound bites.' Few attorneys were willing to take him on, for fear it could adversely affect their careers.

I jumped into the conversation by saying, summarily, we agreed with him, in that a close relationship with the news media was something we should always be aware of. Then I said to Fred Wapner, "Why don't you describe the witness problems you are having in the Hunt case?" That began the one -two punch. As Fred stated it, the entire case hung by a thread, involving this one witness who was petrified that the defendant could have him eliminated. The DA's Office had gone to great lengths to have him put in a Witness Protection Program where his identity had been changed. If the TV cameras showed his photo to the world, his life would definitely be endangered. Also, if there was full TV coverage, the intimidation might cause the witness to be dissuaded from testifying. Fred explained this witness was critical in two murder cases and, if he refused to testify, it was likely the house of cards would all collapse in these homicide cases.

Fred made it clear he wasn't opposed to TV coverage of the courtroom. He halfheartedly joked about how important TV had been to his family. His dad was Judge Wapner, the judge on the ***People's Court*** TV program, and at that time he was the most well-known judge in the country. That comment tended to defuse the situation. Fred, in his typical serious style, explained how everyone was concerned with what Joe Hunt might do. He was out on bail and in contact with many of the BBC members who could either harm the witness or put pressure on him not to testify. This was a heated debate that could have ended badly had it not been for the team effort by the prosecutors from the Santa Monica Office. They had made a compelling argument to make an exception.

I could see the DA wanted to satisfy the news media by appearing to be open-minded and not obstruct them from covering publicity cases. I wanted to find some common ground that would please the media but not jeopardize the prosecution of the case. Along those lines, I was aware that the media wanted to be present during the so-called 'Hovey' jury selection. The Supreme Court in the legendary *Hovey* case had ruled that both sides had a right to examine potential jurors ***in private***. The theory was that jurors would be more candid in answering controversial questions if done in private. In this way, the other jurors wouldn't be able to hear the juror's answers. This was all new law, and the judge in this case indicated that the 'Hovey' questioning should be held in private, which excluded the *news media from being present during the questioning of the prospective jurors.*

My suggestion was, why not give the news media the coverage in the questioning of the jurors? This would then make the DA's Office appear to be in favor of 'transparency.' In other words, give the media something while at the same time object to full TV coverage, especially of our key witness. I could see the DA was interested in pursuing this idea. He was a pragmatist who knew the art of negotiating and compromising. The prosecution team continued to make a compelling case against the TV coverage. That's when I noticed the DA looking at his watch, indicating this hour-long meeting had reached its zenith.

The meeting was concluded with the DA saying he wanted to consult with some of his staff and he would have an answer for us in a couple of days. I was pleased with Fred Wapner's presentation and how vigorously he had pursued the issue. It would have been great if the DA had completely sided with the deputies, but at least he didn't slam the door on them.

Two days later, I received a phone call from the DA's Office. I was told that the DA had given Fred the authority to object to the TV coverage of the key witness if he decided that it was in the best interest of the case. At the same time, the DA encouraged Fred to see that the news media was included in the Hovey jury selection process. As it turned out, we were able to protect our witness while at the same time giving the news media something they wanted.

The Joe Hunt case continued to generate problem after problem, requiring me to step in and find solutions. During the four-month trial, I was constantly being called by the prosecutors for approval on various legal issues. Much of my time was consumed with providing resources for investigators to travel to various locations to check out sightings of the missing victim. When you read the story of the Joe Hunt case, you will see how difficult it was to prosecute a 'No Body' case, as the Defense continued to claim the victim was still alive and had been seen at various places in the country. We couldn't afford to chase every sighting story. However, there was one that needed to be checked out, and I was willing to provide the resources for an investigator to travel to Tucson, Arizona, in order to explore the possible sighting of the victim at a service station, especially since this sighting occurred two years after the shooting. I knew the Defense was going to call two witnesses who would claim they believed they had seen the victim there. We checked it out thoroughly and found no credible evidence the victim was alive and well in Tucson.

However, the Defense came up with more sightings, some in Monaco and others in Rio de Janeiro. I had to make decisions as to how much taxpayers' money we should continue to throw at something we couldn't disprove. As to sending investigators out of the country, I decided to draw the line. To me, that would have been a waste of money. However, many others disagreed with me. These are the kind of tough decisions that have to be made, even though they may be unpopular to others who say don't spare any expenses on a case.

My point in this INTRODUCTION is to explain to you, the reader, that I thoroughly know the inside story of what happened in the **Billionaire Boys Club** cases because I lived it. However, my knowledge of the **Menendez Brothers** was from a different perspective. My assignment had changed since it was the 'post' O.J. Simpson era. After the unfortunate outcome in the O.J. Simpson case, I was asked by the then-DA, Gil Garcetti, to create a Trial Support Division, which would provide visual and technical research assistance to trial attorneys in presenting their cases to juries. I accepted the challenge and wanted to see what services would be helpful to prosecutors who were involved in big cases.

By the spring of 1995, I had converted part of the DA's Library for the basis for my new Division. At that time, the DA's Office was gearing up for the second trial of the **Menendez Brothers.** David Conn was selected to be the new prosecutor. Years before, I had worked closely with him on a Death Penalty Manual. Without a doubt, he was the most knowledgeable person on murder cases that I had ever come across. When he got the assignment of the Menendez case, he came to me in Trial Support and asked me to assist him in researching several legal issues that had arisen in the first trial. David and I did extensive legal research and came up with several appellate cases that would completely change the course of the second Menendez Brothers jury trial.

When David and his assistant, Carol Najera, started the second trial in August of 1995, they were so well prepared that the Defense was caught off guard. Besides having a near-photographic memory, David remembered some obscure cases and could recall them when he needed to use them in his legal argument. I admired David and enjoyed working alongside him.

As a result, I became aware of all the witnesses and facts in the Menendez Brothers case. I remember when David was ready to argue the case he wanted me to prepare courtroom charts showing each witness and listing their level of credibility.

Every lunch hour he would call me from the courthouse in Van Nuys and tell me what he needed prepared for the next day. I would work on his project all afternoon, and at the end of the day an investigator would pick up the visual aids and transport them to the Van Nuys courthouse. The next morning, David would walk into court with his new charts and continue with his argument. He was so focused and organized that it was a pleasure to watch him take apart the Defense Argument, layer by layer.

I am getting ahead of myself. What I wanted to convey to you, the reader, is that I was very much involved in both the **Joe Hunt - Billionaire Boys Club case**, as well as the **Menendez Brothers** second trial. Often True Crime writers have to resort to hearsay on hearsay since they didn't have the opportunity to actually live the trials from the inside out. This INTRODUCTION is to provide you with some perspective of where my knowledge of these events comes from.

Since I am now retired, I have had the opportunity to reflect back on all the cases I had been involved in. I was the only person who had such direct contact with BOTH these extraordinary cases. What was puzzling to me about Joe Hunt and the Menendez Brothers was how could these human beings, who had been given so much, turn into cold-blooded killers?

While working on both cases involving rich kids who became killers, I had to think back to the notorious **Loeb and Leopold** case from the year 1924. As a child growing up, I remember hearing about that case during high school. It was hard for me to envision how these two super-rich kids from Chicago could plan and carry out a crime of kidnapping for ransom of a 14-year-old, Bobby Franks. I found it was so ruthless how these two rich kids could kill a young boy, not for the money but just the mere fact that they wanted to commit a 'Perfect Murder' and get away with it.

These killers had no conscience and killed to prove they were Superhuman and above any man-made law. The **Loeb and Leopold** case was so similar to the **Joe Hunt** and **Menendez Brothers** because they were, in both cases, rich kids who believed they were above the law and with their superior intelligence would never get caught.

The Loeb and Leopold case made me recognize that the phenomenon of Rich Kid Killers isn't anything new. There seems to be a pattern in such killings that I felt compelled to write this book to uncover what drives and motivates the RICH KID KILLERS OF BEVERLY HILLS.

CONTENTS

CHAPTER 1 BUSINESS MEETING

June 6, 1984, was a memorable date for many reasons. It was a brisk, gusty morning when President Ronald Reagan stood in front of a stone monument at Ponte de Hoc in France, overlooking the beaches of Normandy, to commemorate the 40th anniversary of D-Day. He turned to the elder WWII veterans with graying hair, seated in military straight rows before him. He exclaimed to all present and watching on TV how brave these American Rangers had been when they climbed ropes and ladders to ascend the cliffs behind him to launch the liberation of Europe. During the battle, these soldiers recognized that desperate situations required desperate measures on their part to overcome the German soldiers firing down at them from tucked away in the concrete bunkers above the bluffs.

On that same day in 1984 in Beverly Hills, a young man by the name of Joe Hunt was faced with a desperate situation. His business, the Billionaires Boys Club (BBC), was on the verge of ruin. Joe realized it would take desperate measures to save his BBC organization. To reach his objective would require the snuffing out of a human life, which was an obstacle in his way. Joe was facing herculean challenges. All his tireless effort in creating the Billionaires Boys Club had made him one of the most talked-about young business leaders in and about the City of Beverly Hills. But like many business ventures, what goes up often comes down with a thundering thud.

Many rich and successful entrepreneurs are able to ride out a crisis because they have savings that can tide them over until business improves. However, Joe didn't have the option since he was not born into affluence and had nothing like a safety net to catch him if he fell. He needed money now, a large transfusion of cash. He could think of only one person who could immediately supply the funds he needed. That man was **Ron Levin,** who lived in Beverly Hills. Joe had worked with him on various investments in the past and had learned Ron had stashed large amounts of cash in several Swiss bank accounts.

Consequently, Joe had developed a plan in which he would meet with Ron at his home in **Beverly Hills** so they could discuss future business ventures. In order to create a cordial environment, Joe stopped at a fancy bistro on Wilshire Blvd. and picked up some delicious takeout food. His selection of entrees proved to be perfect for the occasion. The evening started out with a few drinks, and the pleasant meal followed. Their discussion centered around how to make money with the least amount of effort on their parts. Both men were exceptional schmoozers who could be extremely convincing. They prided themselves on having the talent to be consummate salesmen who knew how to 'Close the Deal.'

Around 9:45 p.m., while seated and enjoying an agreeable conversation, there was a muffled sound originating from the rear door. All of a sudden, a black man burst into the room with a huge gun in his hand. He shouted out orders to Joe Hunt that he was there to collect on the money he owed the Mob. Proceeding over to Joe, he placed the gun against his temple and said something about blowing his head off for not paying what he owed. Joe tried to calm the threatening situation by placating the man with the gun. Joe didn't hesitate to admit that he owed a significant amount of money to the underworld as a result of his losses from his Chicago commodities trading. Joe had been stalling the mob with the claim that he was about to receive a large amount of cash from Ron Levin. Joe wanted Levin to feel the pressure, since he had told people that Levin owed him several million dollars from the commodity project they had earlier embarked upon.

The gunman didn't exhibit any interest in hearing about excuses and continued to wave the gun around, demanding the money or else someone would be shot. Ron Levin didn't know what to make of this situation. He felt it was like an old B movie of a Hollywood Gangster era, one in which he didn't have a role to play, except for the fact that all the action was unfolding in his living room. As the tension intensified, Joe started to beg for time in order to obtain the money he was about to receive from Levin. The gunman seemed to become more threatening and made an ultimatum that he wanted the money NOW.

Joe was on his knees pleading for just a little more time. Then Joe slowly turned to look over at Ron Levin, who had slithered into a corner of the room trying to make himself less conspicuous. Joe, in a most contrite voice, asked if there was anything that he, Ron, could do. Ron didn't know how to respond since he had the feeling that he was an outsider who didn't have any 'Skin in this Game.' Then Joe made a desperate plea to Ron, asking if he could loan him some money to save his life. Joe hastily promised he would be able to pay it back the next week when a big deal closed. As Joe sluggishly got up off his knees, he suggested to Ron that he could write a check on one of his Swiss bank accounts.

Like a light bulb clicking on, Ron interjected that he could write a check on one of his accounts. But how much would be needed to satisfy the man with the gun? Joe said that about $1½ million should be enough. He then asked the man with the gun if that amount would be sufficient, and the guy nodded his head, as though it would take care of the situation for today. The gun was removed from Joe's head to give the three of them some breathing room. Next, Ron indicated that in order to provide the funds, he first needed to retrieve a check from his desk in his office where he kept his checkbook for his Swiss bank accounts.

Ron escorted everyone to his office, where he reached into a bottom drawer and removed a Swiss checkbook. He sat down at his office desk and asked who the check should be made payable to. That was when some self-doubt was expressed. It would seem strange to make a check out to an organization like the 'Mafia.' Joe spoke up, stating the check should be made payable to 'Microgenesis of North America, Inc.' in the amount of one million five hundred thousand dollars. Joe said he could endorse it and the Mafia could cash it. Ron Levin placed the check in his typewriter and filled out all the required information on the Swiss Credit Bank check. Under Payer Levin typed in his name, Ronald George Levin KKL 620.76-32-001.

When Levin was finished, he handed the check to Joe, who scrutinized the completed check to make sure everything had been filled out properly. Levin remained at his desk with his checkbook full of blank Swiss checks. Joe took the filled-out check and handed it to the gunman for his review. Then Joe said these fateful words: "Do you think we should have asked for more?" At that moment in time, Levin cocked his head and looked directly at Joe with the most dumbfounded look of surprise, which soon faded to shock.

CHAPTER 2 WHO WAS RON LEVIN?

Ron Levin was a person who wanted to live in Beverly Hills. This city consists of two types of people, those who have made it and those who want to appear to have made it. Santa Monica Blvd. cuts like a knife directly through the city. Those residing above the line have made it, and those below are mere wannabes. Ron Levin's house was definitely south of the tracks; his Beverly Hills zip code of 90212 wasn't the exclusive 90210, but it was close enough for him. He also had the benefit of being within walking distance to the exclusive shopping area of Rodeo Drive.

When one tries to define the difference between an astute stockbroker vs. a "con man," the contrast is often hard to distinguish. Both want to take your money, albeit with your consent, and tell you that they will make a substantial profit for you. When you end up making money, they are a wise broker. But when they lose your money, then they are considered "con men." Ron Levin had been in many business ventures where he had tried to use other people's money which ended in a financial loss. As a result, he gained the reputation to many of being nothing more than a "con man." That designation may not be entirely fair to Ron, but his reputation was tainted by so many sore investors who ended up as losers.

As a matter of fact, Ron had served prison time for defrauding other investors in the past. He was a person who was known for running countless marginal businesses. Ron knew that in order to make money, using someone else's money, he had to appear to have that 'Midas Touch.' Ron was someone who could spot profitable opportunities and quickly act on that information. He certainly didn't broadcast his fraud conviction and only a few, if any, knew the facts about it. He dressed for success and projected the image of being a winner. But most of all, Ron Levine talked a good line, as did Joe Hunt with his Billionaire Boys Club (BBC). Both men were well aware of the importance of projecting the impression of being a winner in order to be successful.

Joe Hunt was experiencing desperate times for his BBC business, in which more funds were being spent than being earned. Who and what could generate money quickly for him without his investor knowing of his dire financial situation? Ron Levin seemed to be the perfect person who had the necessary contacts and skills.

Months earlier, Joe and Ron had an encounter that had a major impact on their personal relationship. Joe was over at Ron's place talking about a business deal when Ron's maid came into the room and interrupted the two of them. The maid said to Ron, "It's the Police Commissioner on the phone, and he wants to know if you have arranged for Muhammad Ali to attend the Children's Hospital fundraiser." Ron responded to the maid by saying, "I worked that out this morning, so tell the Commish he will be there." Later, Joe told other members of the BBC how impressed he was with Ron Levin's connections and influence. (There was no such charity event. Ron Levin would use his maid to set up these little white lies just to impress his visitors.)

As to this earlier business deal, Ron listened with interest to Joe's proposal, but he wasn't persuaded to put any money into the BBC investments. Joe was more than desperate, so he kept pestering Ron. Finally, Ron stated he would give Joe an opportunity to prove himself as a shrewd investor. Ron said he would set up a commodities account at his brokerage house with a line of credit of five million dollars. Joe's name would be authorized to make trades on this account. The agreement was if Joe made money for Ron Levin then the two of them would split in half the profits. To Joe, this seemed fair in that he would be using somebody else's money in an attempt to make money for himself.

Joe made some contacts with several long-standing colleagues in the commodities business and received tips on several exceptional buys that would soon come on the market. As a result, Joe started making trades with the Ron Levin's brokerage house. Slowly, the account generated a profit. Joe's unpleasant memories he had encountered when he first worked on the Chicago Mercantile Exchange kept him from straying too far into risky investments. Years earlier, Joe was willing to take risks in order to make a killing in the commodities market since there wasn't as much at stake. But now the future of the BBC was in jeopardy, and he couldn't afford to make any careless mistakes. Every investment was carefully assessed as to risk and profitability. Ron Levin had thrown Joe a lifeline, and he and the BBC were going to sink or swim, depending on Joe's ability to pick the winners in the commodities world. For Joe, it was like playing the tables in Vegas, but with caution.

Joe knew all the fast and loose talk wasn't going to help him in building this account. He made the usual investments that were easy to turn $5 million into $8 million. But to reach a high profitability, he would have to make some calculated gambles. To outsiders, Joe projected a 'wheeler and dealer' image, but his inner circle of friends believed Joe possessed a sixth sense that only he could comprehend. With a certain trepidation, he made several gutsy moves that bounced the account up to $12 million. Joe was ecstatic with this success, but he also wanted to do something even more impressive by tripling Ron Levin's account. He talked Levin into giving him a little more time, which Ron was willing to do. At that time, Joe knew he had only a limited amount of time to prove his genius. Joe gazed at the list of commodities and grabbed anything and everything he could get his hands on to read. At this point, it was like 'reading tea leaves' in an empty cup. He had never worked this hard to figure out the market, but he felt the pressure on him to get this right. The final date was days away, and he bought several more commodities he thought were underperforming. It was like rolling the dice and hoping Lady Luck was looking down on him.

When the time was up, Joe met with Ron Levin. He was so excited to show Ron that he had taken the $5 million and rolled it into $14 million. Although he wasn't able to triple the money, he had come very close. Joe was more than euphoric with his success in his trading efforts in Levin's account. Joe told the members that he had made slightly more than a $4-million-dollar profit on the Levin account. In other words, the Levin account was going to save the day so no BBC investor would suffer a loss.

When Joe asked Levin for his $4 million in profit, Levin told him the proceeds were tied up in a shopping center he had purchased in Chicago. Levin tried to appease Joe by telling him that a Japanese investor wanted to purchase the shopping center, thus the result would be an increase in profits exceeding $30 million. Joe had a meeting with the BBC members and indicated there would be a short delay, but the new profits would be distributed to all concerned. Joe had figured out how to distribute all the proceeds. Joe, Dean Kelly, and Ernie Daly (pseudonym) would get a million each, while the Robinson brothers would receive $700,000.00.

Because of all the excitement, Joe couldn't wait any longer and contacted Levin's commodities broker as a way to speed up the payout to him. He made some inquiries about the account, and the broker admitted there was no money in the account and it was all made up. The broker said that several months before he had been contacted by Ron Levin, who had said he was doing a TV documentary. Further, Levin had told the broker he needed an account set up because they wanted to compare who did the best in trading commodities—such as a clever guru like Joe Hunt, a computer, or someone just throwing darts at a board. In other words, Joe was merely playing a part in a TV documentary.

When Joe found out he had been played for a fool, he was madder than a wet hen. He was humiliated that he had been made a chump in the eyes of the BBC members. The strangest part of Joe's misperception of Ron Levin was that he had honestly believed Levin was independently wealthy. Apparently, this was based on Levin having stacks of bank passbooks reflecting large deposits. What Joe didn't know was that Levin had made up all these passbooks on his own just to impress people. So, Joe told his close friend Dean Kelly he wanted to stay on the good side of Levin because someday he was going to get his money from Levin and ultimately kill him for revenge.

CHAPTER 3 WHO WAS JOE HUNT?

Trying to describe Joe Hunt is not an easy task. His true name was Joseph Gamsky. He could truly be called 'special' since he was born on October 31, Halloween in 1959. Could that explain his devilish ways? He grew up in the San Fernando Valley, an area experiencing turbulent growing pains in the 1960s. It was a suburban area that consisted of more than a third of the City of Los Angeles.

In 1797, the Catholic fathers created a settlement named Mission San Fernando Rey de Espana, which was ten miles north of downtown L.A. Originally, the land was used for dry crops such as wheat, but then in 1913 the Los Angeles Aqueduct was built to bring water from the High Sierra Nevada Mountains to the booming City of Los Angeles. The appellate federal courts ruled that all the water from the aqueduct could only be used on the property within the Los Angeles city limits. That was when all the small cities in the San Fernando Valley, which were desperate to receive the aqueduct water, decided to annex to the City of Los Angeles. The result was that Los Angeles doubled in size.

After World War II, the San Fernando Valley became the center for motion pictures, automobile, and aircraft manufacturing, which resulted in the construction of thousands of new homes. As Joe Hunt was growing up, so was the San Fernando Valley developing, with dozens of shopping centers and housing tracts going up. During the 1970s, the valley was also becoming the center of a multi-billion dollar pornography industry. It soon became the nation's largest adult video and magazine distributor. Its nickname during this time was 'San Pornando Valley' or ***'Silicone Valley'*** for the increase bust size, not to be confused with the other ***Silicon Valley*** (in Northern California), referring to computer chips.

Joe and his brother went to the local public schools. Both were gifted students and did well academically. Joe's teachers found he was not only brilliant but also possessed an uncanny maturity, far above his age group. His teachers noticed how important it was for Joe to be the best at whatever he set his mind to do. Even if it meant he had to do a little lying or cheating in order to win, that didn't seem to bother him.

Joe's father could best be described as a 'free spirit.' He made his living as a storefront psychologist and was often seen riding around town on his motorcycle. His father required Joe to call him by his first name, Larry, and wanted to be thought of as a teacher more than a dad. The emphasis was to make the boys as self-sufficient as possible. Joe learned the importance of impressing others. He went out of his way to expand his vocabulary so he could drop words to amaze and captivate his peers. He used words that baffled the other students to prove to them that he was someone exceptional.

The turning point in Joe's life was when he and his brother won scholarships to the prestigious Harvard Prep School located off of Coldwater Blvd., near Studio City. It had been a boys' military school, but by the 1960s the emphasis was on being a prep school instead of being a military institution. The prominent families of

Hollywood had their sons attend the new Harvard Prep School. Some of the noted families included sons of Darryl Zanuck, Gregory Peck, Charlton Heston, Roy Disney, and even Jerry Lewis. It also included the sons of the 'Rich and Famous of Beverly Hills" who attended Harvard Prep. When 12-year-old Joe entered the hallowed halls of Harvard Prep with his free scholarship, he didn't emulate the usual rich-kid image as the others.

He didn't have the money the other boys had, nor was he invited to attend the social parties the rest of the students enjoyed. Joe's dad knew this school would be the key to his son's success since it was ranked as one of the top prep schools in the country. How do you compete with the richest of the rich kids in town? He didn't have a chauffeur who picked him up after school, but he had to use public transportation, which he caught on the corner of Ventura and Coldwater Blvd. He didn't wear the latest fashions from Rodeo Drive. Besides those setbacks, he was a six-foot-tall, lanky nerd type who just didn't fit in easily.

Many remembered him as the straight 'A' student who read the congressional record during lunchtime. He tried to adapt and ran for all the student government positions but lost every election. Joe was self-conscious and felt like an outsider. However, there was one place where he excelled, and that was on the debate team. He was gifted when it came to speaking. Even at this time in his life, he wanted to be on top. The other students had to admire Joe for his nimble debater's mind. Yet even though he became the star debater, he was dismissed from the team when it was found he had falsified evidence during a debate tournament. For Joe, even at an early age, winning was everything no matter what the cost.

The opportunity for Joe to attend Harvard Prep gave him the chance to associate with and know the kids from the families of the Rich, Famous, and Powerful. As time went by, he cultivated some friendships with the other students by helping them academically. Although the other students didn't include Joe as part of their group, they recognized he was exceptionally gifted and they were not. Later on they would come to appreciate his business acumen and want to follow him in order to appear to be successful.

On the following graphic page there is information about Joe Hunt's background.

Graphic 1

JOE HUNT
BILLIONAIRE BOYS CLUB

Joseph Gamsky
Later Joe Hunt

ORDINARY VALLEY BOY

- Name- Joseph Gamsky
- Born San Fernando Valley
- Grew up in tract house
- Father store front psychiatrist
- Mother left family
- He was tall (6') & skinny

Harvard Prep.

Chicago Mercantile Exchange

Many of the Rich Kids
Lived in Beverly Hills

Bombay
Bicycle
Club

BILLIONAIRE
BEVERLY HILLS
BOYS CLUB

Name of Group

Bombay Bicycle Club to BBC to Billionaire Boys Club

CHAPTER 4 JOE LEARNING ABOUT BUSINESS

By the age of 19, Joe Hunt had graduated from Harvard Prep School and was headed to USC. His supposed graduation in only a year and a half was questioned by some, but he claimed he challenged certain exams and the university was forced to bestow a degree on him. Others dispute his explanation and believe he just dropped out and never graduated from USC.

What is known as a fact is that after a year he wanted to do something stimulating, so he studied for the Certified Public Accountant (CPA) exam. Based on his ability to study and his exceptional memory, he found the accounting material easy to comprehend. When he took the CPA exam, he passed with flying colors. He boasted that he was the youngest CPA in the country. With that feather in his cap, he became a commodities trader at the Peat, Marwick and Mitchell brokerage house in downtown LA. After six months, he realized he didn't fit in and quit. During this period, Joe became reacquainted with Dean Kelly and Ernest Daly, his old friends from Harvard Prep, who were then attending UCLA across town.

He had proved to himself that once he put his mind to something he could be successful. By 1980, Joe's father and mother divorced, and his dad decided to relocate to Chicago. Joe followed his dad and became engrossed in the financial dealings at the Chicago Mercantile Exchange. The hectic pace of the buying and selling commodities fascinated him. He leased a seat on the exchange and realized how quickly money could be made. It wasn't long before he gained a reputation as a bold trader whose investment strategies paid off.

He convinced his old buddy from Harvard Prep, Dean Kelly, to talk his family into loaning him $400,000 to invest. For Joe, this was what he had been waiting for to prove to others at the Exchange—that he had developed an exceptional method for investing. Joe was meticulous in each of his moves and made sure that he steadily increased the investment. It wasn't long before he had piggybacked the money to over a million dollars. The Kelly family was impressed, and the people working at the Exchange were astonished.

It then appeared that Joe had the magic touch as the money spiraled to several millions. As the size of the pot grew, Joe became more emboldened, taking more risks to build the pie larger and larger. Other dealers at the Exchange became suspicious of Joe's wheeling and dealing, and some eyebrows were raised. Ultimately, he ran the Kellys' modest investment of $400,000 to $14 million in a period of 18 months. Like everything in the commodity market, what goes up always comes down. The only question was how quickly can you hit bottom? For Joe, the $14 million evaporated into thin air within weeks.

As for a double whammy, Joe was suspended from the Mercantile Exchange. Of course, he wanted to blame 'organized crime' and others for his downfall. It later was uncovered that Joe had taken various investors' money and had failed to register that money in their names. As a result of not playing by the rules, he was suspended for 10 years from the Exchange. Joe was smart enough to head out of town, leaving his dad to live alone in Chicago.

The only place he knew anyone was in Los Angeles, so he returned in hopes that he could start over. When he arrived in LA he had only four dollars in his pocket, meaning he was dead broke. He had no place to stay, so he contacted his old friend, Dean Kelly, who allowed him to move in with him. (Note to reader: remember the name Dean Kelly, since he was the one TRUE friend to help Joe when he was down and out).

This humbling experience was most difficult for Joe. He had to reflect on what went wrong, and that was when he developed a new philosophy to life. Since he didn't have any money to start over, he had to rely on others to help him out. How could he convince others to give him money when he had nothing to show for his business ventures in Chicago?

He had a bold idea of creating an investment organization that would attract the Rich Kids of Beverly Hills to follow him. It could be said that Joe Hunt would become the **Pied Piper of Beverly Hills**. He wanted to form a group of intelligent, capable, and motivated young men who could succeed in business as well as all their personal and social ventures.

He wanted to show them it could be done without the usual type of constraints and intrigues associated with the long climb up the corporate ladder. In other words, they didn't have to spend years working their way to the top. His approach would permit them to start at the top and remain on the top forever.

CHAPTER 5 GENESIS OF BBC

The year was 1984, which was a year everyone had been waiting for. Since 1949, the public had been waiting for this year to occur because of the highly popular book titled ***1984*** by George Orwell. It was a political science book predicting what the future had in store for the public. Orwell described a world where everyone's life would be controlled by Big Brother. The government would dictate everything in a person's life. The ministries' names were antonymous doublethink to their true functions: The Ministry of Peace concerns itself with war; the Ministry of Truth with lies; the Ministry of Love with torture; and the Ministry of Plenty with starvation.

What was ironic about the book *1984* was the fact that Joe Hunt operated the BBC in a very similar manner. Joe would say that black was white and that white was black. His 'Paradox Philosophy' was very Orwellian in its structure and content. Joe was one who knew how easy it was to control a person's mind by changing words like Orwell did in his notions of "Newspeak" and "Doublethink."

Strangely, when the year 1984 did occur Joe Hunt was using many of the Orwellian methods to manipulate and control members of the BBC. He was a master at controlling the members. His philosophy consisted of a combination of situation and utilitarian ethics, meaning 'the end justifies the means' in that one should do whatever was necessary to benefit oneself. Everything depends on how one looks at each situation. A person has to be willing to do anything, as long as there is a payoff at the end. In order to carry out his philosophy, one had to understand that the impediments between what you have and what you want are external, not internal. One needs to free oneself from the concepts like good and bad or true and false. His thinking made one realize it was possible to approach the same situation from an infinite number of angles.

Reality was "circumstantial," and you need to re-orientate one's perspective so you could always see things in the way that best suited your needs. The philosophy called for the group not to be inhibited by society's rules of law and religion. The survival of the individual was the sole end. A person has to be ready to commit crimes, even murder, which would be justified under the 'Paradox Philosophy.'

Joe knew that he had to have a catchy name for his organization. When he was working in Chicago, he hung out at an establishment frequented by young professionals called the Bombay Club, which was referred to as the "BBC." He realized the West Coast crowd wouldn't be impressed by that title so he changed it to the ***Billionaire Boys Club***, evoking a sense of exclusiveness and entitlement. By 1984, he was ready to expand his investment club to more than his close friends. After his fall from grace in Chicago, he had been considering an idea on how he would establish such a group. The purpose of the club was to supply funds for Joe to invest and then he and the others would gain from the profits he made.

The BBC was a new type of organization where the structure was not important, but it focused on the merits of the individuals. A member would need no more than an idea to create his own company, financed by Joe through his commodities trading.

The BBC was structured with 30 or so prospective members, set up in cells, comprised of a small number of members and a nexus of communication between the cells. These cells would propose investment projects that would be presented to the whole club for it to decide which ones they would invest in. Joe and his cronies, Dean Kelly and Ben Daly, would be at the top and be called "Shadings" who operated in the shaded realm since they were the ones well versed in the 'Paradoxical Philosophy.' They would resolve any disputes that might arise.

Joe wanted to bring in young men from wealthy families who always wanted to impress their parents but never could because they didn't know how to be successful. In 1984, the BBC had an enormous appeal for young men, and a group of them began to meet regularly. They were in their early twenties, the sons of men whose money and influence they could only **hope to inherit** but were **unable to duplicate.**

To qualify as a member, Joe would give each of them a test which was eccentric but was a way to graphically explain his philosophy in order to be successful. He would ask each potential member the following:

"Would you murder someone, if you knew you could get away with it, for a million dollars?"

The person would respond, "No."

"Would you do it if it were a matter of saving your life?"

The person would generally say a hesitant, "No."

"Would you murder someone if you had to do it to save your mother?"

Then the person gives a confusing "Yes."

"Then you can't claim that you have a line you won't cross."

What Joe was trying to convey was there aren't any moral absolutes but, if it came down to believing sufficiently in a situation, one would have to be willing to take the necessary action. The rich kids of Beverly Hills couldn't match Joe's wit on how he could turn things inside out. They were mesmerized by his charismatic manner. He had a gift for telling a story that rich kids could totally relate to.

Since Joe had grown up with so many rich kids, even though he wasn't one of them, he knew what they wanted and what they couldn't achieve on their own. He knew how to fundamentally get through to the rich kids, and that was through flashy cars, gorgeous women, and fashionable living. What Joe could give them most of all was recognition by their parents and family that they were capable of being successful at a business, just like their dear old dad.

What Joe did was give them titles to their own company, such as CEO or vice president in charge of sales. The mere printing up of business cards with fancy titles gave these rich kids the first chance to show others they were truly valued. It didn't matter that the company was a shell, as long as their title put them on top, which was all they needed to prove their worth to others.

CHAPTER 6 SUCCESS OF BBC

Joe was always looking for something that would be a "get rich quick" investment. Through various ventures, Joe had learned about the Attrition Mill, which was an enormous metal cylinder capable of reducing ore to ultra-fine powder that could then be separated into precious metals. It had been invented by a Gene Burns (pseudonym) at his desert plant in Hesperia, CA. He was a biochemist who had spent nearly 18 years trying to develop a machine that would have all sorts of uses to quickly and effectively reduce ore to valuable metals. Joe recognized the potential of this machine and thought it was a matter of salesmanship and developing efficient manufacturing of this product that could result in colossal profits. Joe made a deal with Burns that the BBC would give him a salary, a house, and a car in return for the rights to improve and market his machine.

Joe set up a meeting for all the BBC members to drive out to the high desert in Hesperia to see the machine in action. Burns, the inventor, was impressed with Joe. What fascinated him the most was when the BBC members drove into his plant's parking lot in a parade of luxury cars consisting of Mercedes, Rolls Royce's, BMW's, and several Porsches. He couldn't help notice that most of the drivers and their passengers were in their early twenties. Joe was trying to amaze the developer of the 'Machine' while at the same time trying to show his young followers that he had a sixth sense in finding investments that were ripe for the picking with the possibility to make a fortune.

The rich kids from Beverly Hills recognized this could impress their parents, illustrating how bright they were at uncovering business opportunities. Joe didn't have any money of his own to invest in this new device, but the rich kids of Beverly Hills did. He gave a sales pitch on how he was going to change the name of the device to the 'Cyclotron,' and he had buyers waiting in six of the western states. All he needed from his associates was some money to invest in the production of the Cyclotron. The rich kids who drove out to the desert to look at this investment agreed to put up whatever money was needed to make it happen. Most of the kids had been given these luxury sports cars, so they took out loans on their cars to come up with the cash to start the BBC investment in the Cyclotron.

For the young men, it was a painless way of investing because they had borrowed money on their cars and continued to drive them, just like before. They felt like geniuses figuring out how to make money out of thin air. They were happy, the inventor was happy to have his invention marketed, and of course Joe was happy since he was able to bring this all about by smoke and mirrors.

It didn't take long for Joe to realize his BBC members were natural experts in one particular business. Each one of these young men knew practically everything about luxury cars. They knew which were the fastest, most fashionable, and the most expensive. Ever since these rich kids were twelve years old, they were talking about cars and what they wanted to drive when they grew up. The luxury car market was an area they were born into and understood better than most people.

Joe, through his contacts, met a businessman named Steve who had access to "gray market" luxury cars imported from Europe at less than half the price they could be sold for in California. Joe recognized how lucrative this business could be, so he set up the West Cars of North America. He was able to provide the company with more than a quarter of a million dollars in assets by persuading other BBC members to sign over their own cars as collateral. This was the easiest business for Joe to set up since the members knew what they were talking about and also knew so many people who were in the market for luxury cars.

However, the bread-and-butter business of the BBC was the commodities market, which of course was Joe's field of expertise. He created the Financial Futures Company, which he used for his trading at the Beverly Hills brokerage house of Cantor, Fitzgerald & Company. All the accounts were set up in the names of Tom Robinson (pseudonym), Dean Kelly, and Alex Gravely (pseudonym). Even though Joe had been suspended from the Chicago Mercantile Exchange, there was no difficulty for him to continue to do commodity trading using others' names. Joe's selling point was that he promised an investor a high rate of return with little risk. To make it appear like money was coming in, he sent out to the investors a financial statement and personal dividend checks to show how much they had made on their investment.

Basically, Joe had three separate businesses that comprised the business side of the BBC. He needed office space where he could operate all three businesses under one roof, so he leased space in a building on Third Street in West Hollywood. It was a moderate size office building in which he leased one entire floor. To make the place impressive, they spent $100,000 for software in the conference room and another $30,000 to stock the BBC's law library.

The offices were remarkable. Each member arrived at the workplace around 10:00 a.m., leaving enough time to return calls until noon. Then from 12:00 p.m. to 2:00 p.m. they entertained potential clients over lunch, returned to the office a little after

2:00 p.m. and handled any new accounts, then left around 3:00 p.m. The members liked the business hours because it didn't interfere with their very active social lives.

The following graphic page shows the various businesses that the BBC invested in.

Graphic 2

CHAPTER 7 PONZI SCHEME FALLS DOWN

Joe, with the help of the BBC members, was convincing the rich to invest in the BBC investment pool, called Microgenesis. The new investors were thrilled by the high return the BBC investments yielded. At the beginning, when the investors received their hefty dividend checks they were so impressed they would then give the dividend check back to Joe for reinvestment. Of course, the investors were so ecstatic with the high return they would tell others who would want to invest their money with such a profitable group.

As time went by, things began to change. If someone invested $100,000, they believed that all of their money would be placed in investments with high returns. Over time, Joe was placing only half the funds received in commodities, with the other half used to pay off the earlier investors and pay for the BBC personal expenses. As long as there were new investors, the investment scheme did well and no one complained. However, when the number of new investors started to dry up, a cash-flow issue arose.

Joe could be described as being glib when this problem surfaced. He said that the Cyclotron was about to go to market. What was true was the tests on the Cyclotron were very promising and it was only a matter of ramping up production to have them ready for delivery to the buyers. Another large investment company, United Financial Operations Inc., was looking for another investment company to acquire. There were discussions they might buy up the BBC, once the sales started coming in on the Cyclotron project.

In Beverly Hills, there was a buzz about Joe Hunt, this 26-year-old whiz kid, who was making money hand over fist. From the sport car agencies to the fashionable eateries, the talk of the town was that Joe Hunt had a knack for making easy money. The fanfare was overwhelming, and everyone wanted to invite him to lunch or dinner in order to pry out of him the secrets of making fast and easy money. He was the Jim Cramer, Suze Orman, and maybe even the Donald Trump of the 1984 era.

Nonetheless, during this time Joe, Dean Kelly, and Ben Daly were huddling together to figure out what to do about the new critical cash shortages that were occurring. Joe's companions were whistling the famous tune from 1984 by Hall and Oats, ***Say It Isn't So***. Joe admitted to Dean that capital formation was the most delicate part of business. Joe was keenly aware he had built a house of cards mandating the need for a perpetual insertion of money to prevent the house from collapsing.

What Joe had learned in his business ventures was that the image was more important than the reality. So Joe knew he couldn't afford to cut back on his excesses. It was the illusion of prosperity that kept the new funds coming in. But now ALL of this new money went directly for the glitzy parties, stylish Italian suits, elegant Rolexes, and sporty Ferraris. Nothing was going into the commodity company for investment purposes because it was all being spent at the front end.

Joe had created one of the largest PONZI schemes ever seen in Beverly Hills. As of that moment, only Joe knew the end was near if the BBC didn't receive an immediate transfusion of money.

CHAPTER 8 CARRY OUT PLAN

Joe had confidence in his ability to carry out any task, whether it was making millions or committing murder. Still, he wasn't the type who was cocky and kept everything in his mind. Joe was the first to admit the need for notes or lists to make sure every task was done in the right order to guarantee complete success. DON'T LEAVE ANYTHING TO CHANCE. So, even with this simple little business meeting with Ron Levin, it was complete with a well-orchestrated list. The hit TV show in 1984 was Angela Lansbury's series ***Murder She Wrote,*** which might explain why Joe had to write out every step of his murder plot.

Joe's list of things that had to be done in order to successfully kill Ron Levin is as follows:

1. Tape mouth
2. Handcuff
3. Put gloves on
4. Close blinds
5. Scan for recorder
6. Kill dog
7. Put answer service on 668
8. Get alarm access code
9. Date stamp documents & letters

10. Make file of letters & other material

11. Use corporate seal

12. Have Levin sign Agreement & fill in blanks

13. Xerox everything so he has copies

14. Xerox authorization

Each one of the items had a specific meaning to Joe. It was a reminder of what he needed to accomplish. The one about "kill dog" was meant to be used if the victim, Ron, wasn't willing to cooperate, in which case they would threaten to kill the dog that the victim adored. There were additional items on the other pages such as "get alarm code," "pack a suitcase," and "keys." All of them were to make it look like Levin had left on a trip to N.Y. On one of the pages it stated, "Jim digs pit." This was done the day before, when Jim Powell (pseudonym, Head of Security for the BBC) and Joe went to Soledad Canyon to dig a grave. That was when Joe complained to Jim that they had picked a place where the soil was too hard to dig a deep-enough grave.

Joe had rehearsed with Powell that when he would ask him if the amount of Levin's check was sufficient, Powell was supposed to say "No, What else have you got?" That would give Joe a chance to squeeze more money out of Levin. Unfortunately, Powell didn't pick up on the hint. So when Joe asked, "Is that enough?" Powell casually stated, "Yeah, that's fine." Joe was mad as hell at Powell for screwing up the one line he was supposed to say.

When that was said after the Swiss bank check was given to Joe, Ron Levin began to think. It was at that point he realized he had been set up by Joe Hunt, a true con man. At that moment in time, Ron Levin glanced up at Joe, and when he looked directly into his cold, calculating eyes, he understood he had been scammed. That was when Joe started checking off items on his list. They pulled out the handcuffs, followed by taping Ron's mouth shut. Next, they pulled out the gloves and put them on as they perfunctorily walked over to the blinds and gently closed them. The next phase of their plan was to look for a phone recorder and put the answering service on 668 (calls go directly to voicemail).

By this time, Ron had several moments to reflect on his possible fate. His reaction was to start crying. The sobbing became louder and uncontrollable. The so-called hit man, Jim Powell, motioned for Joe to move Ron into the bedroom. The three maneuvered into the master bedroom, which was located at the rear of the duplex and would be the quietest place. The moment of truth had arrived for Joe Hunt. Did he have the resolve to kill another human being? He had planned everything out to the minutest detail. Nothing could go wrong. He had succeeded in obtaining the 1½-million-dollar check that was going to save the BBC. Ron Levin had fallen for his phony story about a Mafia hit man was after him. He had to be pleased that all his planning was paying off.

Ron Levin was face down on his bed as Powell held a .25 caliber pistol with an attached silencer. Powell waited patiently for the prearranged signal from Joe to do the dastardly deed. When Joe had finished reviewing the list, he smiled at the thoroughness of his organization. His head turned in Powell's direction and he gave the nod, which was followed by a muffled bang. Powell shot Levin in the back of the head. Joe heard Levin's last breath, like an explosive gasp. Blood started seeping out of the wound, so they quickly wrapped Levin's body in the bedspread on the bed. Accidentally, they wrapped the TV remote control in the bedspread and took it with them. He observed Ron's body twitched slightly and then there was no more sobbing or movement emanating from Ron's lifeless body.

On the following graphic page are photos of Ron Levin's house as well as the check that Levin gave to Hunt.

Graphic 3

JOE HUNT
BILLIONAIRE BOYS CLUB
Ron Levin
Joe Hunt
Jim Powell
Ron Levin's
House
Levin's Body
placed in trunk
of his car
SWISS CREDIT BANK
ANNULLIERT
FOR COLLECTION
Swiss Bank Checks
bounced for lack of
funds

CHAPTER 9 GETTING RID OF THE BODY

Joe was meticulous in his planning of the murder, but he was even more thorough in making sure he would be able to get away with it. There was no delight in organizing the perfect murder unless you are 100% sure you could get away with it. That's what makes it a flawless crime. So their initial task was to get Ron's body out of the house without being seen by the neighbors. Obviously, one would wait until it was dark, just not too late at night when it might cause people to wonder who was making all that noise.

Inside the house, they had decided to wrap the body in the bedspread/comforter on the bed. They had to roll the body several times to get it to fit inside the large comforter. The master bedroom was near the rear door, thereby minimizing the distance the body had to be carried. Joe went outside and drove the car into the alley, then pulled it into the back courtyard, stopping near the back door.

Powell prided himself on the fact that he had earned a black belt in karate. But even with his fitness, he still needed Joe's help to lift the rolled comforter with Ron's body and carry it out the rear door. They tried to be as nonchalant as possible, flinging the comforter in the trunk of the car. It took a little maneuvering for the body to fit in the trunk. Joe walked up and slammed the trunk closed. Unfortunately, part of the body didn't completely fit in, so when he slammed the trunk closed it slightly bent the trunk lid.

So far, everything on the list had been completed on schedule. They wanted to make it look as though Ron had left for a business trip to New York, so they removed a small suitcase and placed it in their car.

In the heart of Beverly Hills, there aren't many good places to bury a body. Joe had thoroughly analyzed the situation. An amateur killer would possibly have dumped the body in the nearby Hollywood Hills. However, that might not be the best place since there are so many curious hikers and sniffing dogs that frequent the area. There was always the idea of dumping a body in the large Pacific Ocean. But Joe was too smart to fall for that approach because, no matter how many weights are tied to the bodies, unfortunately they tend to pop up at the most inopportune time.

Joe realized in the Los Angeles area the best dumping ground for bodies was on the way to the Mojave Desert, which is a mere 60 minutes from downtown L.A. Along the way there are many isolated canyons and dry riverbeds. When Joe was growing up, he had gone hunting with his friends in Soledad Canyon. What amazed him about the area were its vast stretches of nothingness. Subconsciously, he thought this would be an excellent place to dump dead bodies because there was no one around for miles, especially back in 1984.

After they had cleaned up Levin's place, they slowly and quietly pulled their BMW out of the courtyard into the rear alley. From there they headed up to Santa Monica Blvd. and turned left. They passed the wide "Avenue of the Stars" as they drove by Century City, where the moguls of the entertainment industry conduct their business dealings during the day. Joe had dreamed that one day he might have an office in one of those penthouse suites.

But tonight's job was to get rid of a dead body in the trunk of his car. When they approached the 405 Freeway, they entered the northbound onramp. As they gained speed, they crossed over always-busy Wilshire Blvd. They could glance down at the Veteran's Cemetery, where thousands of white crosses were all perfectly lined up in rows. Joe and Powell's minds didn't reflect how many of those crosses were placed there for soldiers who were killed on this day of June 6, 1944, exactly 40 years earlier. Joe's thoughts were on the burial of Ron Levin, not the graves of all the veterans.

Their BMW was humming up the 405 Freeway, and within minutes they were dropping down into the San Fernando Valley, providing them with a dazzling view of the city lights of the Valley. They couldn't believe how light the traffic was this late at night. Joe's thoughts zoomed back in time to when he grew up in this Valley.

As his nostalgia faded away, they had crossed the entire Valley and were now approaching the turnoff for the 14 Freeway. They veered to the right, placing them on a lonely freeway heading to the High Desert. As they continued, very few lights were visible. Finally, they saw the turnoff for Soledad Canyon Road. They maneuvered down the off-ramp and went a short distance to where they turned onto a narrow dirt road. There they traveled for a mile at a snail's pace over a bumpy road filled with potholes. It was pitch dark, and the only illumination was coming from the headlights of their car. Not a living soul was anywhere in sight.

Joe understood the importance for the body to never be found. The story would be Ron Levin, the con man, had moved on with his life. There were a number of law enforcement agencies who were already investigating Ron Levin for various forms of fraud. Joe wondered what would be the best way to make sure that if his body was ever found it could never be identified.

After they had made a sharp turn, they spotted the tree where they had dug a shallow grave the day before. They pulled to a stop and backed the car up to the grave. The trunk was opened, and the pungent odor from the dead body hit their noses. After gasping for fresh breath, they both grabbed a portion of the comforter and pulled the body out of the trunk. Because of the weight of the body, they both had to drag the comforter within inches of the grave. They could see the grave needed to be enlarged. They then took turns digging with the shovel. After several feeble attempts, both men concluded that grave digging wasn't their calling.

In order to make sure the body could not be identified as Ron Levin, they reached into the trunk and grasped a shotgun. (This was in 1984, before DNA became a forensic tool.) They placed the hands to the side of the corpse and started blasting away at them so there would not be any fingerprints that could be used for identification purposes. Then it was time to concentrate on shooting at the victim's head so there wouldn't be anything recognizable. When they shot the back of Levin's head, his brain matter blew out of his skull, landing on his chest.

Most people would have been horrified at seeing the bloody cerebellum landing on a person's chest, but for Joe there was a half a smile, almost like saying, "Well, I'll be damned." Joe was pleased with himself when he realized he was the epitome of his 'Paradox Philosophy.' So far, his thorough planning had paid off. They mustered up some more energy and dug the grave deeper, making it more difficult for anyone to find the body. Joe had remembered to bring along a bag of lye and covered the body all over with it to make it quickly deteriorate. After filling in the grave, they then placed boulders all across the top to ward off any wild predators from digging it up.

By now it was late, and both men had had a full day. They packed up their shovel and shotgun, placing them in the empty trunk. They climbed back in the car and gunned the engine. The rear wheels spun, spewing gravel all over the grave. Then it was back to the highway and home. With the Swiss bank account check safely placed in a folder, they felt the entire ordeal was definitely worth 1½ million dollars. This check was truly the lifeline that would save the BBC.

CHAPTER 10 COVER-UP

The next morning, Ron Levin was discovered missing in a peculiar sort of way. Blanche, Levin's housekeeper, had called Levin's house at 6:00 a.m.to make sure he was up, since she had agreed to take him to the airport for his flight to New York. She didn't receive an answer, so she went to his house. There she met Ron's two traveling companions, who were waiting outside the house. The housekeeper had a key and let everyone inside. They looked in every room and couldn't find Ron.

This was all odd, since the security alarm wasn't on, the blinds were down, and the dog was acting peculiar: nothing was adding up. Further, the airline tickets were still there with his Luis Vuitton luggage, and his black toiletries case was still in the linen closet. The housekeeper spotted several other strange things in that a pillow, a sheet, and a bedspread were all missing. The TV remote control for the bedroom was also gone. The master bed had been remade with the guest room comforter, not his usual comforter. On a kitchen table were cartons of take-out food with only a few bites missing.

Everything seemed so creepy because his car was in the garage, but his wallet and keys for the house and car were missing. The housekeeper called Levin's mother to come over. When his mother arrived, she noticed the answering machine had not been answered. She said it was his custom to check it first thing whenever he came into his house. Based on all the peculiar findings, Levin's mother and his friends went directly to the Beverly Hills Police Department to report all these suspicious facts. Could it possibly be a murder? Since murders are so rare in Beverly Hills, the police discounted that possibility right away. The police indicated that unless there was blood on the walls, there was no reason to suspect murder, and as to filing a Missing Person report, police said everyone usually shows up in a couple of days.

Joe was far more than brilliant. He was a genius, or the closest thing to one. The reason for the timing of the incident was that Ron Levin was planning to travel to New York. In order for a Perfect Murder to be complete, Joe wanted Ron's credit card to be used on the east coast. So Joe decided that it would be Jim Powell's task to be a decoy by going to New York and using Levin's credit cards. For Powell, this was the fun part of a perfect crime since he got to travel, stay at fancy hotels, and dine at gourmet restaurants. No need to consider the price of drinks; he could just order whatever he wanted because he wasn't paying for it.

The plan was, after Powell checked out of the hotel he would leave Ron's wallet, containing his identification and credit cards, in one of the alleys to make it look as if Ron had been mugged in N.Y. and possibly been the victim of a crime.

After spending several days in the hotel, Powell went to check out using one of Ron Levin's credit cards. The bill was for several hundred dollars, and it seemed like it was taking considerably longer than usual to square the account. The cashier explained they were having some difficulty running his credit card through the system. Up until that moment, Powell had been having the time of his life running up a tab on the credit cards.

An assistant manager finally came up to the counter and stated, in a very quiet voice so others nearby couldn't hear, "Mr. Levin your credit card has reached the maximum limit and can't be used until paid down." Hotel personnel came to the front desk, and Powell was suddenly surrounded. He was asked, very politely, if he had another credit card he could use. Powell began to wonder what to do. He could use one of his own credit cards, but that could implicate him in the disappearance of Ron Levin. He thought he had some cash, but that totally would defeat the purpose of traveling to NY to lay a paper trail of Levin's travel there.

Powell started to sweat as his mind was churning at a hundred miles an hour. He was thinking, where was Joe when he needed him? The agreement at the BBC was that Joe was the brains and he, Powell, was the muscle. Powell was trying to buy some time; however, the hotel staff was starting to question the situation. Powell was definitely an African-American and didn't fit the name Ronald E. Levin on the credit card, which had a Jewish ring to it. What added to their suspicion was the fact that he was traveling without any identification having a photo of him on it.

Powell had left his luggage in his room, so he waited for a moment. Then when the clerk walked away, he discreetly headed back to the room. The clerk had notified security to come to the front desk. When the clerk noticed that this "Levin person" had left the reception desk, he told security, and they took off in pursuit of him. Powell was fast, but he wasn't familiar with all the passageways in the hotel. The chase didn't last long. Powell had gone down a dead-end hallway. Security caught and held him until the police arrived, handcuffed him, then took him to the station.

Powell was petrified of the situation in which he found himself. The police certainly weren't looking at him as a murderer but as a flakey person who was using someone else's credit card to pay a hotel bill. Then he made a phone call to Joe. It wasn't a pleasant phone call either, since Powell was mad he was in jail and the fact that Joe had not anticipated that Levin's credit cards were 'maxed out.' Joe wanted to blame Powell for botching the job he had been assigned. Eventually, they both realized going through the blame game wasn't going to solve their immediate problem of getting Powell out of custody. Joe may have been a knowledgeable businessman, but he was unfamiliar with the criminal justice system.

Immediately, Joe was on the first plane to N.Y., where he headed to the courthouse. Joe had seen a new TV series in 1984 called ***Night Court,*** in which Harry Anderson played a judge who worked late dispensing justice. Joe took a taxi to the courthouse and looked for anyone in a business suit. He saw a man fitting that description with a briefcase walking down the steps of the courthouse. Joe walked up to the man and asked if he was an attorney. The man continued walking, apparently afraid he was going to be served with papers.

Joe was persistent in following the man, who begrudgingly admitted he was an attorney. Joe held up $700 in cash and waved it at the man, who at the sight of the cash turned and said, "How can I help you?" Joe quickly exclaimed he had a friend by the name of Ron Levin whom he wanted to get out of jail. Joe said the $700 was for his lawyer fee plus $ 2,000 for Levin when he was released and $2,000 for the Plaza Hotel where Powell had been staying under the name of Ron Levin. The attorney did his job and Powell, aka Ron Levin, was out of jail and on a flight back home to L.A.

Joe's idea of creating a massive Ron Levin footprint in Manhattan had been a disaster. The police now had a black man, claiming to be Ron Levin, as well as Powell's mug shot with the name Ronald Levin under it. Was the perfect crime starting to unravel? Only time would tell.

CHAPTER 11 CASHING CHECK

Joe didn't need this distraction in New York since his main concern was keeping the BBC moving forward before a catastrophe could strike. He was pressuring some of the rich members to find new sources of money to prop up the sagging financial picture. All would be well within the next several days, since by then they would have an additional $1½ million in their bank account. As soon as Joe arrived back from New York, he went to the bank to cash the check signed by Ron Levin.

Joe had opened an account at the World Trade Bank in an effort to expedite the cashing of Levin's check, which was drawn on a Swiss bank account. The operations manager of the World Trade Bank submitted the check to Credit Suisse in Zurich on June 8. Everyone was happy, and the bank VP told Joe it would take several days to clear the check because it involved a check on a bank in another country. Joe could wait a few days in order to get the transfusion of new money pumped into the BBC. Everyone was upbeat since this was going to turn the corner for everyone involved. The money would be used to help several members with their investments since they needed some 'seed' money. The bank would be able to make some loans on projects that were already in the hopper.

On June 15, Joe received a telex from Credit Suisse stating the check was dishonored due to insufficient funds and a missing signature. This shocked Joe, as all their great plans were being derailed. Joe had to believe this was a mere mistake and that the check was on the wrong account, since Ron Levin had numerous Swiss bank accounts. Did the account have a balance slightly under $1½ million?

Joe directed Powell to arrange to have Levin's Swiss bank send new blank checks to Levin's post office box. The idea was to write several checks on various accounts to see which one had the funds deposited in it. The bank was just as excited as Joe was in making the check good. This would look good on the bank's monthly ledger sheet.

Everyone was eager to get the green light in order to have the money to start flowing into BBC accounts. It was only a mere formality and everything would be back on track. Joe at times could be impatient, but this time he had to be patient with so much riding on the money from the Swiss bank account. After waiting for almost a week, he was tired of phone calls to the bank and continuing to receive the run around. Joe went down to the bank to talk to the assistant manager to find out firsthand what was causing all the delays. When he got to the bank, the assistant manager asked to meet him in his private office at the back of the bank. The banker opened a folder and showed Joe the Swiss bank check. On the back was the word "ANNULLIERT." Above that was typed "A, 14.6.84 zur Zahlung vorgelegt und nicht bezahl. Zurich, 15.6.84"

Joe had a surprised look on his face and said, "What does all that mean?" The banker said they had tried to put the check through several times and it always came back indicating "**INSUFFICIENT FUNDS.**" The bank manager advised Joe they contacted the Swiss bank and they had stated the account had a balance of **only $49**.

The banker went on to say that maybe the account holder wrote the check on the wrong account. He suggested Joe call the account holder and find out if there was another account that had the money. When the banker motioned to Joe he could use the bank's phone to call the account holder, Joe caught himself before saying, well that would be impossible since I just killed him.

Joe's face turned pale. As he stood up, he seemed to have lost his balance as he staggered out of the bank. The banker didn't know what to say except that he could put the check through again if he found out the money had been put into the account. Joe wanted privacy to collect his thoughts. He went to his car, sat down, and closed the door. All he could see was the smiling face of old Ron Levin as he said, "You can't Con a Con." Joe shook his head and thought, how could **Ron Levin have conned him twice**?

Joe had two problems he had to address. First, who could he trust with this news? The other was how to prop up the image of the BBC without sufficient funds coming in. He figured the BBC expenses were running $70,000 per month, but he wasn't bringing in that amount in new investments. In the financial world, this is called a cash flow issue; others might call it a liquidity problem.

Joe called a special meeting of eight members he felt he could absolutely trust. He related to them how he had tested each one of them as to what was their limit for killing another human being. He told the group, "Jim and I knocked off Ron Levin." He then explained all of their money had been lost and that in order for the BBC to survive, he had had to kill Levin. He went on to say to the group that "it was a perfect crime" and "there is no way in which we would be caught." He gave them a pep talk that they still had some money and resources and a lot of good projects. He assured all eight members they could get back on their feet if everyone stayed together and worked diligently in generating funds.

Since he was concerned that there may be some defections, he added the following: "If anybody talks to the police they will end up in the East River and become fish bait." It was a strange statement to make in that there was no 'East River' in Beverly Hills, but apparently he remembered it from an old gangster movie that was based in New York.

He explained he had to kill Ron Levin in order to save the BBC. Telling it to them meant they were now all involved in the murder. This came as a shock to several members who were just along for the ride, including the parties, and then pretending they had a productive job. However, they hadn't signed on to being **MURDERERS.**

Joe then announced the BBC was going to hold the most magnificent party to exceed all other parties. He encouraged these members to make sure to invite any rich kids they knew who had money. That weekend was billed as a greatest party ever. The excitement grew as Saturday arrived. The BBC knew how to put on parties. It was important to have the right place, gourmet food, an open bar with no limit, and a DJ who knew how to groove. But most of all, no shortage of gorgeous babes, barely covered, with low cleavage and shortest of short skirts. The name of the game was IMAGE, and Joe needed to make it appear he was "Putting on the Ritz."

In order to reward his BBC members for their patience and dedication, Joe gave each one of them a new motorcycle. The members were ecstatic and the wannabes were ready to join up. First, a few had to take their new toy for a spin. Fortunately, no one was hurt with all the drinking and racing around on their new bikes. Joe knew his "Boys," and this was a morale booster the BBC members needed.

Besides helping some bruised egos, the biggest accomplishment of the party was that a young man by the name of Tasa Eslaminia (pseudonym) had been invited. He was so impressed that he wanted to join as a new member. His claim to fame was that his father was a rich Iranian who had been a high-level official in the government of the Shah of Iran. After the fall of the Shah, Mr. Eslaminia had deposited his millions of dollars in Swiss banks and immigrated to America, the land of opportunity.

Joe had a chance to talk with Tasa and found him anxious to fit in with all the others. Tasa explained that he and his father had a strained relationship, which was a common theme among most of the members. He indicated his father had tons of money but he didn't freely hand it out to his son. Joe was intrigued with the endless wealth possessed by the father, supposedly estimated to be over $30 million. In that moment of desperation, Joe couldn't help himself from devising a new plan to extort money from Tasa's wealthy father.

CHAPTER 12 MISSING PERSON REPORT

The parents of Ron Levin were growing concerned because they hadn't heard from their son for more than a week. They knew he had plans to go to New York, but he always stayed in contact with them, even when he traveled. They continued to check his house. As time went by, Levin's mother became even more concerned. She had called everyone she possibly could think of who might have been in contact with Ron. Nothing materialized and she was at her wits end. Ron's parents finally returned to the Beverly Hills Police Department and asked them to issue a Missing Persons Report.

The police took the report, but the detectives had information that Ron Levin had a prior conviction and the DA's Office had recently filed felony fraud charges against him. One detective said to the parents, "This isn't the first time a 'Con' has left town when being investigated." That was not the reassurance his parents were looking for. The detectives knew there were quite a few people looking for Levin and maybe he realized it was time for him to leave town.

As the weeks drifted into months, the police became more concerned and started an investigation. They checked his house out, especially the business transactions he had papers on: in particular, his investment into Microgenesis. They checked his mail, which didn't indicate anything unusual. When they checked his message machine, they found a number of people who had continued to call him, asking him to return their calls. There were several calls from a Joe Hunt, who wanted Ron to call him as soon as possible regarding his investments.

Ron's parents and the police didn't know where to turn for information about his whereabouts. The police looked at Missing Person cases quite differently than family and friends of people who go missing. Often the police give little attention to Missing Persons reports. In most cases, the missing person reappears within two weeks. Most situations involve a person wanting to get away from parents or partners in a relationship ready to move on. A few are spur-of-the-moment situations in which a person meets someone and just decides to run off with them to have a good time or make a clean start somewhere else. Other situations are where a person leaves on a vacation or a business trip and doesn't notify all the people they should have contacted.

When the police initiate a Missing Persons investigation, they need to understand something about the missing person's personality and lifestyle. Very few situations are indicative of a criminal situation such as a kidnapping or inflicting possible harm on others. When the police were looking at the Missing Person Report on Ron Levin, it was hard to categorize what type of case it was. None of the usual red flags appeared as they do in most cases. The police made the usual contacts with the coroner, hospitals, and the New York Police Department, but nothing materialized.

Ron's parents were concerned enough to pick up the mail and check his yard for watering and putting the trash out. One day his father, Martin Levin, wanted to tidy up the ultra-clean house. He took all the business papers and placed them neatly in a folder. He came across a yellow tablet that contained seven pages. What made it peculiar was that it didn't look like Ron's handwriting. Whose writing was it, and what was it doing in Ron's house? It looked like a list with the words at the top "At Levin," "To Do." Other things on the list were CLOSE BLINDS; TAPE MOUTH; HANDCUFF; KILL DOG.

Mr. Levin was about to throw the papers in the trash but stopped himself and reflected that it was easier to save them than to be scolded by his son when he returned. But he began to have an uneasy feeling about everything. He thought there must be an explanation, but he figured he wasn't thinking clearly, so he threw the yellow tablet in the stack of business papers he was saving in the folder.

The Missing Persons investigation wasn't getting much attention because there were no clues or leads to be checked out. Levin's parents tried to think of the names of people the police should interview, but they couldn't think of anyone who should be talked to.

The following graphic page shows the location of the Beverly Hills Police Department with the To Do list that was found in Levin's house. Also, there are photos of Soledad Canyon where the body was buried.

Graphic 4

JOE HUNT
BILLIONAIRE BOYS CLUB

Soledad Canyon where bodies were buried
but never found

CHAPTER 13 NEXT PLAN TO GET MONEY

Putting aside the disappointment Joe was experiencing, the fact was his financial situation was beginning to deteriorate. It is like a shark attack: when the faintest scent of blood drops in the water is when sharks start circling their prey. The word had gotten out that the BBC was delaying payments on the dividends. Joe and the others tried to spin it as a mere technical glitch that would be fixed by the end of the month. They said it was just a matter of dealing with the growing pains that were being ironed out.

At that moment, Joe would have grabbed at any idea to gain money for the BBC. Tasa, an aspiring member, claimed that his father had absconded from Iran with millions. Joe didn't care whether Tasa's father had $30 million or only one million. He only saw it as a way to save the BBC from insolvency. Tasa further claimed that his father had his money stockpiled in Swiss bank accounts. Joe had just encountered negative vibes from a Swiss bank account that had only $49 in it. One would think

Joe would be highly reluctant to get involved with another Swiss bank. But it might have been Joe's desperation that forced him to pursue the situation.

Joe checked out Tasa's dad and verified that he had escaped with a huge fortune. The Shah of Iran, Mohammad Reza Pahlavi, was considered the wealthiest man in the Middle East. He wanted to modernize Iran, which at that time was the world's largest oil producer. Sadly, he clashed with the Muslim religious leaders. Eventually, a revolution consumed the country and the infamous 'Black Friday' occurred on September 8, 1978, in which the Shah's government tried to quell the riots by shooting into a crowd, killing many of the protestors. This was the final blow to his government, and he was forced into exile in Egypt. Many of his government leaders realized that once he had gone into exile they had no protection from the religious extremist groups, so they also left the country. Tasa's father's name was Hedayat Eslaminia, one of the high leaders who was able to escape. Like the Shah, Hedayat had moved his money into Swiss bank accounts so he could continue to live well outside of Iran

Once Joe knew for sure that Hedayat had large amounts of money, he began trying to figure out how he could obtain part of that fortune for the BBC. His idea was to convince this Iranian political exile to sign over part of his assets to his son, Tasa.

Joe came up with an extortion idea, which he referred to as "Project Sam." He had learned Hedayat was living in Belmont, a small city near San Francisco. The plan was to kidnap and transport him to Los Angeles, where he would be tortured by Joe until he was willing to sign over some of his holdings. The unanswered question was, what they were planning to do with Hedayat after he signed the documents?

Joe and some of the other BBC members had verbally stated to Hedayat's son, Tasa, that his father would have to be killed in order for the plan to be successful. Tasa never seemed to comprehend the logical conclusion that his dad would end up dead. Joe selected only the members he felt he could trust to carry out the plan. This included Dean Kelly, Ben Daly, and Jim Powell. Tasa was brought in and advised that he was to supply certain information, but was not going to participate in the actual kidnapping.

It was July 30, 1984, when the plan was put into motion. The first thing that had to be done was for Dean Kelly to rent a house bordering Bel Air and Beverly Hills. Kelly had told a real estate agent that he needed a secluded house where his friend, who was an author, could finish a book he was writing. The house they rented was well isolated from any neighbors where they wouldn't be able to see or hear anything that took place at the house. This house was ideal for their needs. They could easily torture Hedayat into signing documents and checks without creating any noise.

Dean Kelly flew to San Francisco to join the other members. (Remember, this was pre 9-11, when you could run into an airport to catch a flight without being screened by TSA security). From the airport, he hailed a taxi that drove him to the Villa Motel in San Mateo, where the other members were waiting. The plan was to enter into the Davey Glen Apartments where Hedayat Eslaminia lived so they could kidnap him. The challenge was how to do all this without creating any suspicions or any possible witnesses to their kidnapping.

Initially, the plan involved the gents being dressed up as police officers, making an official call to his apartment. There they would make it appear as if they were arresting Hedayat and transporting him to the police station. However, the more they discussed that plan, there was concern as to how they could transport him. None of them had vehicles that looked like a police car, nor could they easily rent one. Joe was reluctant to go with the police decoy plan since he thought it could create too much attention. They were trying to come up with a plan that would blend into the ordinary surroundings.

They had noticed delivery people were constantly delivering and picking up packages. One of the members suggested they could dress as UPS delivery men. No question that UPS deliverers are the most recognizable in their Pullman Brown uniforms. As a delivery company, UPS has been operating since 1907. They use the same type of trucks, without any vehicle labels, manual transmissions, no power steering, and no radios. Many people wonder why so many of their drivers wear shorts and always have their doors open, which can be explained by the fact their trucks don't have any air conditioning.

This delivery service idea had a lot of possibility, in that Hedayat wouldn't be suspicious of opening his door to a UPS delivery man. They could make it look like they were delivering a large package to his apartment. Once they were inside the apartment, they could put a rag soaked in chloroform on his face to knock him out. Then they could place him in a steamer trunk and carry him out to the truck.

All the guys were proud to have contributed to such a great plan. Joe said he could use his dad's truck, which had a camper shell on the back. Dean Kelly indicated he would take on the tasks of picking up the UPS uniforms just before he rented the house in Bel Air where they would take the victim. They reflected, to themselves, what a smart group of dudes they were to figure out such a sophisticated kidnapping plan.

When Kelly arrived at the Villa Motel, all the guys were given their new UPS uniforms. They had purchased two old steamer trunks and had covered both of them with butcher paper. They went so far as to write Hedayat's name and address on the butcher paper. This would be a good decoy and would explain why UPS needed four guys to make the delivery.

By 3:00 p.m., they were ready to set their scheme into motion, with Joe driving his dad's truck and the others following in a BMW. They left San Mateo and headed to Belmont where the apartment complex was located. It was a short distance, only a couple of miles to the apartment. They pulled into the public parking area, and the guys jumped out and slid the wrapped-up steamer trunks out of Joe's truck. They were all neatly fitted in their UPS uniform. As they carried the steamer trunks to the apartment complex, everything looked perfectly normal. They proceeded down the walkway to Hedayat's apartment. They rang the doorbell and waited. They knew he was home, but it wasn't clear if he was alone. The other trunk they were carrying contained their kidnapping tools, but it could be used to carry away another occupant if he wasn't alone. They waited and waited but no one came to the door. What should they do? Abort the plan and come back another day, or continue to wait? Then there was some slight sound from inside.

CHAPTER 14 SAN MATEO KIDNAPPING

Joe was dreading any delay since he felt the pressure to immediately procure the money to save the BBC. Just as two of the guys turned to leave, the door lock made some noise. One of them loudly stated, "UPS delivery, we need a signature." Then the door was opened a crack and they could see inside the figure of an older gentleman. They stated the boxes were heavy and they would bring them in. Hedayat was surprised and didn't know exactly what to do, so he stepped back; this gave the guys the chance to enter. Hedayat had backed into the apartment and when the last UPS guy came in he closed the door.

Immediately one of the guys grabbed a chloroformed rag and held it over Hedayat's nose and mouth. The old man struggled a little, not knowing what was happening to him. The rest of the guys knew their assigned tasks and went to work. The victim was quickly handcuffed so he couldn't break free. The chloroform wasn't knocking him out like they thought it would, so he started to struggle and make noises. Joe decided they needed to get him into the empty steamer trunk and close the lid to prevent any noise that might arouse the curiosity of the neighbors.

Everything was left in the other trunk since they weren't going to need it. Then the moment of truth came: Who would be able to carry the trunk out with the victim in it? Jim Powell was a black belt and certainly could do his part in carrying the heavy trunk. Joe had the most at stake and was by far the tallest of the other guys. Joe and Powell picked up the trunk and sort of stumbled out of the apartment door. The victim was inside the trunk, moving around and trying to make noise. The guys carried the trunk out as swiftly as they could as beads of sweat dripped from their new UPS hats.

When they got to Joe's dad's truck, all of them helped lift up the boxy steamer trunks and slid them into the camper shell. Joe looked around to see how much of a commotion they had created. He couldn't see anyone looking at him, so he told everyone to get back in the car and truck and go to the local U-Haul truck rental yard in San Jose.

U-Haul is one of those American success stories in which Sam Shoen of Ridgefield, Washington, founded his company in 1945. He began building rental trailers and splitting the fees for their use with gas station owners, who he franchised as agents. This business grew like mushrooms on steroids, and eventually U-Haul started renting trucks. Joe had selected U-Haul because they were one of the few that rented trucks with a **one-way** service. Joe had no desire to return the truck all the way back to San Jose, so that was why he decided on U-Haul trucks. Most likely Joe was thinking of the 1968 Dionne Warwick song titled "Do You Know the Way to San Jose." He knew the way to San Jose but had no desire to return.

They rented a 12-foot truck with a covered cargo bed. Joe and the others checked the truck out to make sure it could make it all the way to L.A. It seemed okay, although it had a few dents and scratches on it, which Joe had the clerk acknowledge on the inspection report. They drove it around the block and backed it up to Joe's dad's pickup. The guys pulled the steamer trunk, with the body in it, out and slid it onto the bed of the U-Haul truck. This would make it easier to transport the victim.

As anyone knows who has ever rented a U-Haul truck, there is a mixed feeling when starting off driving a rental truck. It makes you feel all-powerful driving a big truck. However, there is another side of you who feels the weight of the responsibility when maneuvering a big vehicle on the narrow streets. They went through the usual routine of adjusting the side mirrors to better see any vehicles behind or to the side of them.

It was time to make the 600-mile trip to Los Angeles. Joe drove his truck, and Dean Kelly's job was to ride in the bed of the U-Haul truck with the steamer trunk. The entire idea was to transport Hedayat, alive, to the house Dean Kelly had rented that morning in Bel Air. Joe had to be pleased with the precision with which kidnapping had been conducted. Using the UPS uniforms was an ingenious move, and now it was just a matter of time to obtain the signed documents. Then it would be sending Tasa to Switzerland to obtain the money and bring it back in order to breathe new life into the BBC.

When driving from the Bay area to L. A., a traveler needs to make pivotal decisions. Should one travel the old 101 freeway, which is more scenic but a much slower drive, or should one take the super-straight but boring Interstate 5 Freeway? Joe was anxious to resolve this situation as soon as possible, so the three vehicles headed southbound on Interstate 5. This stretch of freeway is thought to be one of the most unexciting drives in California, since Interstate 5 doesn't go through or near any real cities. All one sees is the flat ranch land, sprinkled with a few cattle to make it a little more interesting.

Possibly the only excitement is a pit stop for gas and a cold soda in Kettleman City. This may be considered an oasis to the few who call it home. There is no market or street lights, and some might even say there is nothing there. That's not being fair to this city, since they are proud to have one of the finest Hazardous Waste facilities in the state. Very few other cities could brag about having such a facility. It is strange Kettleman City is one of the few areas of California where the population continues to decrease with every census. What all travelers look forward to is seeing the highway sign announcing, "You are now leaving Kettleman City."

Remember this was July 30, the hottest time of the year for this area. Everyone was enjoying the air conditioning except Dean Kelly, who was riding in the back of the U-Haul truck, which had to be over 100 degrees. When they were renting the truck, there was a large advertisement indicating some of the trucks came with air conditioning. Dean Kelly never had a chance to enjoy the air conditioning in the truck cab since the interior bed of the truck didn't have any. Dean was dripping wet with perspiration. At first he could hear the victim making noise inside the trunk. Then he heard the victim say, "Please sir, please let me out." The victim was knocking on the sides of the trunk to attract attention. Even though the sounds were muffled, Dean could hear the victim gasping for air.

Dean had a screwdriver and started drilling some holes in the trunk to provide more air. Then he heard screaming and was fearful someone might hear the victim so he placed tape over the holes. It was a long drive from San Mateo, so Dean got concerned and opened the steamer trunk lid slightly to see the condition of the victim. Dean saw some movement from the victim's stomach, indicating he was still breathing. Then he closed the lid again while he sat and waited as the truck struggled up the Grapevine. Whenever one travels Interstate 5, the driver dreads the steep Grapevine highway that divides the Central Valley from Southern California. When they reached the top, Joe had everyone pull over at a rest stop.

Joe had noticed the U-Haul truck didn't have any brake lights. This concerned him since they had passed a number of CHP units. He didn't want the CHP to stop the U-Haul for a brake light violation. Now he wanted to place the steamer trunk back in his dad's truck. Before making the transfer, Joe asked Dean to check on the victim's condition. When Dean opened the trunk, there was a strong urine smell and he quickly closed the lid. Joe asked him to do it again and to use a flashlight. Dean stood back then slowly opened the trunk and peered in. He said he didn't see any breathing and checked for a pulse. It was at that point Dean looked at Joe, shook his head, and said, "He's dead."

This fact sent shock waves through all the guys, who minutes before were elated over their clever kidnapping. Joe told Dean to close the trunk and continue driving to the house so they could regroup and determine what to do next. They headed directly to the so-called "Safe House" Dean had rented that morning. When they arrived, they unloaded the trunk and moved it into the house. One of them was in charge of picking up some food, and when it was brought in they congregated around the trunk to eat their dinner.

Joe didn't seem surprised but was definitely disappointed. Now how was he going to get Hedayat to sign any checks or a Power of Attorney? Joe didn't waste any time expressing any sympathy for the death of a father of the newest BBC member. Joe's mind was always working, trying to stay one step ahead of the events. It wasn't long before Joe indicated to Dean that they would just have to forge the signatures.

Then the topic turned to what should be done with the victim's body? For Joe, this was déjà vu. Of course, you head to Soledad Canyon and you plant just one more dead body into the landscape. Joe wasn't concerned with concealing Hedayat's body. He knew the high-ranking members of the Shah of Iran's friends were constantly being hunted down by Ayatollah Khomeini supporters. This time there was no need to use a shotgun to obliterate the victim's fingerprints.

Joe took the body, in his dad's truck, to Soledad Canyon. Dean accompanied him, and when they got high on the hillside, Joe stopped the truck. They had wrapped the body in a tarp so they could pull the body out of the truck bed. Both of them dragged the body to the edge of the steep slope, and with a slight kick the body started rolling down the hill. A smile came over Joe's face and he chuckled to himself as the body tumbled against boulders, bounced off, and continued to roll down until it disappeared in the thick chaparral brush. Dean wasn't used to disposing of dead bodies, and the whole situation, with the smell of death, made him feel nauseous.

Then it was off to see the victim's son, Tasa. They didn't mention what had happened to his dad. Joe told him they needed his help in forging the documents required to get funds from the Swiss bank. In short order, the forgeries were made. Tasa and Ben Daly flew to Switzerland, where they presented the checks to the bank and were able to obtain all the funds that were available and return to give them to Joe.

On the following page is the information about the Kidnapping of Hedayat Eslaminia in the Bay area.

Graphic 5

JOE HUNT
BILLIONAIRE BOYS CLUB

Joe Hunt

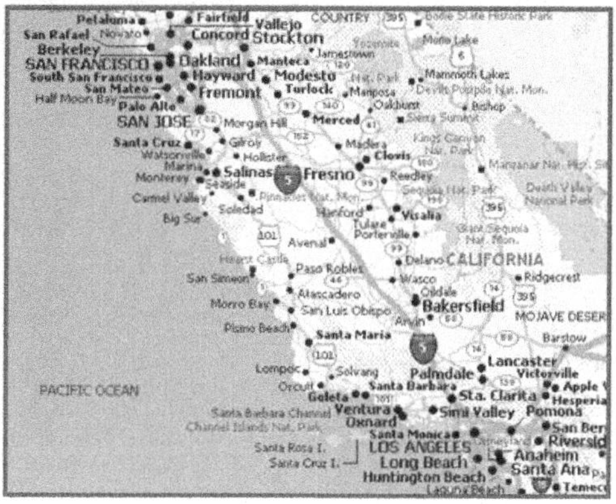

Hedayat Eslaminia

Kidnap & Murder Victim

Kidnapping in San Jose area

They drove U-Haul truck down Interstate 5

They wore UPS uniform to get in apartment.

They rented U-Haul truck

They placed victim in steamer trunk

CHAPTER 15 DOESN'T GO WELL

Joe's world was beginning to unravel. Dean was using his family's money to cover the daily BBC expenses. Joe needed some more time to try to keep the BBC from imploding. He had received some encouraging words that the Cyclotron was about to be shipped to several buyers. Production tests were being run but no money had come in to fill the empty coffers. Joe asked Dean to take a trip to the manufacturing site in Arizona and check on things to see when some money would be received.

The brothers, Tom and David Robinson (pseudonyms), were starting to have their misgivings about Joe. When Tom had learned about the killings, he wanted out. Prior to the killings, David Robinson had related to their dad what Joe was involved in. Their father immediately contacted the family lawyer. Eventually, Tom joined his brother and talked to a Beverly Hills detective by the name of Les Zoeller. After talking to the police, Tom began to make copies of documents he thought would be incriminating.

At this point, Joe became suspicious and didn't know whom he could trust, so he went snooping in Tom Robinson's apartment. Joe discovered a message on Tom's answering machine, and out of curiosity, he played it back. It turned out it was a call from a Detective Zoeller, asking Tom to give him a call back.

Joe now knew that some of his most trusted members had defected. Joe was certain he could trust Dean Kelly and called him to ask him what he had uncovered regarding the deliveries of the Cyclotron units. Joe was declaring war on his estranged buddies and tried to figure out how he could set them up. Joe called Tom Robinson and asked both brothers to meet him at the Cyclotron warehouse, but the Robinson brothers cautiously wouldn't meet with Joe. At that point, Joe professed they were no longer BBC members and he was retaining Tom's pink slip on his car. This title of ownership had been earlier turned over to help finance the BBC. Tom didn't care about losing his car because it was better than losing his life.

Joe met with the remaining members he thought he could depend on. He explained to them that he was planning the murder of a young woman and was setting it up so it would appear to have been committed by the Robinson brothers. This type of talk scared the remaining members. By this time, all the investors in the BBC wanted their money back. Joe immediately set up a meeting with 70 of the investors. He indicated he didn't have their money at that time but he would be able to pay them back soon. He agreed to pay according to a fixed schedule if they agreed not to sue him, as well as give him some time. Surprisingly, most of the investors were willing to give him more time. Their point of view was, what other choice did they have?

CHAPTER 16 INVESTIGATION

The Robinson brothers, as well as some of the other members, were willing to cooperate with the police. Det. Zoeller had received information from several BBC members that Joe may have left his "To Do List" in Ron Levin's house. The detective then obtained a Search Warrant for Levin's house. Det. Zoeller contacted Ron's father, Mr. Martin Levin, who had a key to the house. He asked him to meet him there so he could search for any evidence that may help in the Missing Persons investigation. During his search, the detective found papers regarding Levin's dealings with Microgenesis.

Ron's father wanted to be helpful and told the detective that several weeks earlier when he was looking around for any clues, he had found a yellow writing pad containing seven pages. He told the detective he couldn't comprehend what the papers were about but knew they weren't written by his son. He said it looked like a strange "To Do List." When he handed the papers to Detective Zoeller, the detective's face lit up as though he had just won the Mega Millions Lotto. He glanced at the various items on the list and saw the line stating, 'KILL THE DOG.' He turned to Mr. Levin and said, "This is exactly what I was looking for."

Detective Zoeller couldn't believe what he had. He asked a few more questions of Mr. Levin, one of which was when he had found this "To Do List." Mr. Levin then said he had received a call from a Joe Hunt, who had asked if he could go over to Ron's house because he had left something behind. Mr. Levin said he didn't feel comfortable having someone snooping through his missing son's house so he politely told Joe Hunt, "No."

The police couldn't believe how close they had come to losing this key piece of evidence. Mr. Levin could have thrown the papers out as rubbish, or even worse, he could have permitted Joe Hunt to come over and confiscate the most damaging piece of evidence against him.

CHAPTER 17 FINGERPRINT ON TO DO LIST

On September 28, 1984, Detective Zoeller had Joe Hunt arrested. The two met together in one of the interview rooms at the Beverly Hills Police Station. The detective advised Joe of his Miranda rights and Joe indicated he was more than happy to talk to him. Joe was calm and in total control of the situation. Detective Zoeller told Joe that they needed an exemplary set of his fingerprints. That took several minutes for the Latent Print person to roll a complete set of Joe's fingerprints. They gave Joe a paper towel to wipe the ink off of his hands as the Latent Print person took his prints to the lab.

Joe and the detective continued to talk about Ron Levin, and Joe said that they had been close friends. Joe said, as a matter of fact, the expensive watch he was wearing had been given to him by Ron. Joe wasn't able to explain where Ron might have gone, but he had called him almost every day for over a week. Joe was such a smooth talker the detective was certain he wasn't going to say anything that might incriminate him.

Det. Zoeller excused himself so he could go out and talk to the Latent Print expert to see if he needed more time or if he had been able to compare the latent prints. The expert pointed to the back of the "To Do List" and said there was **one good Latent Print that positively matched Joe Hunt**. Then the detective walked back into the interview room. Joe looked totally self-assured but when he saw the detective carrying in the "To Do List," his face dropped. There was more bad news for Joe, which was that the latent print on the back of that paper matched the fingerprint exemplar he had just given.

Joe glanced at the list over and over, page by page, forwards and backwards. Det. Zoeller asked Joe what he knew about the list, and Joe calmly said, "I don't know anything about this." Joe was no dummy. He knew when to talk and when to shut up. He mentioned to Zoeller that "NOW WOULD BE A GOOD TIME FOR ME TO TALK TO AN ATTORNEY." The detective could see beads of sweat forming on Joe's upper lip. By this time, the detective had Joe's attention. The police needed some time to collect evidence and find any witnesses who would be willing to testify against Joe Hunt. Det. Zoeller let Joe walk out of the station a free man. Joe misconstrued what was going on and believed the police didn't have anything against him, which made him feel even more confident. When he saw Dean Kelly, he told him to work on his alibi for the night that Ron Levin was killed.

Joe's statement to Dean petrified him, in that he feared the detectives might come after him. Joe's most trusted friend, Dean Kelly, went home and explained everything to his parents. Being wealthy people, they knew exactly what to do, and that was to call the family attorney for advice. Dean was just finishing up at Whittier Law School and knew that timing was everything in conspiracy-type cases. The name of the game is whoever gets to the DA's Office first with the most to offer

WINS. In order to save his neck, Dean was willing to testify against Joe and tell everything he knew about both murders. (Remember, earlier it was Dean who was the most trusted person that Joe could rely on.)

Although Kelly didn't play a direct role in the Ron Levin murder, he was present when Joe told eight of the members all the facts regarding the method and manner of the killing. Later on, Joe told Dean that he had gone back to Soledad Canyon to make sure that the coyotes had not dug up the body from the gravesite. As to the Hedayat death, Dean was right in the middle of all the activity. Dean, as a matter of fact, was the person who checked on Hedayat and declared him dead. Dean had the most to offer the prosecution; therefore, the DA was willing to give him complete immunity if he would testify truthfully in both murder cases.

This was a time in Joe Hunt's life when nothing was going well for him. His friends and the BBC members were bailing out, leaving him in the center of this mess. His only hope was that Ben and Tasa, who were in Switzerland, had located some of Hedayat's accounts. That was the good news; however, the bad news was there was barely any money in the accounts. At the most, the total in all of the checking accounts was only a couple of thousand dollars. That amount was barely enough to pay for their airfares to Switzerland. For Joe, it was like the Eurhythmics' (a British music duo) top hit in 1984, ***Here Comes the Rain Again***. Everything that could go wrong was going wrong.

The detectives were aware that Ben and Tasa were trying to obtain the small amount of money out of the Swiss banks. So the police placed an immediate hold on all funds on Hedayat's accounts. This meant that Joe wasn't going to see one dime of this foreign money. Ben's mother contacted him and told him it wouldn't be a good time to return to L.A. Ben and Tasa decided to use false identifications and returned to Los Angeles.

Detective Zoeller felt confident enough to re-arrest Joe, which he did. Joe knew the only chance he had at surviving was to get to the witnesses and dissuade them from testifying. In order to do that, he needed to bail out and meet with these witnesses. Joe persuaded his girlfriend to have her father put up his Bel Air mansion as collateral for his bail. Unbelievably, Joe finessed his way out of jail on a $2 million bail. He was able to continue to meet with people and put pressure on old members of the BBC. This proved to be a major obstacle for the police and the prosecution.

CHAPTER 18 PRETRIAL MOTIONS & MEDIA

The murder of Ron Levin was not a newsworthy story since he wasn't any type of celebrity, just an ordinary con man. Since the DA's Office was prosecuting Levin for fraud, his death would evoke no great sympathy or interest as to the outcome. However, what made the case newsworthy was the fact that all of a sudden a group of Beverly Hills kids were involved in a murder. What stories are newsworthy can best be explained as follows: "Dog Bites Man," there is no story there; however, if it is "Man Bites Dog," now there is a story.

The same is true of a story such as "Rich Kid Killed"; everyone would say, sorry that happened but that isn't an interesting story. However, if it is **"Rich Kids Who Are Killers"**, everyone wants to know more. Since rich kids have everything, they shouldn't need to kill to get what they wanted. No one can say for certain what caused the Joe Hunt case to create so much interest. Some thought it was due to Joe being tall, handsome, and charismatic. Others thought it was the Svengali feature, where he was so persuasive in convincing people to be willing to kill for his cause.

It appeared that this case grew its own legs, in that news media kept following it. By the time the case was ready for trial, all the media outlets wanted to be a part of it. Then came all the requests from the news media, asking the judge for permission to have cameras in the courtroom for the entire trial. The media besieged the judge with requests from CBS's "60 Minutes," ABC News's "20/20," and KCBS Channel 2. Judge Rittenband was fond of media attention. It took on the appearance of a sort of love fest in which there was no downside for the judge, based on the fact the news media has to ask for permission to have cameras in the courtroom. The media are not stupid; they know as long as they make the judge look good they can continue to have access to his courtroom. However, if they are critical of the judge's handling of the case, they may lose their privilege of having cameras in the courtroom. The result is that the media plays up to the vanity of the judges.

The Hunt case was one of the first cases to be tried after the change in judicial policy of allowing cameras into the courtroom. The Judicial System had received criticism for obsessive publicity in two separate cases, five years apart, in the 1950s. The ***Dr. Samuel Sheppard*** case and the ***Dr. Bernard Finch*** case involved doctors who were charged with killing their wives for the nurses who had become their mistresses. In the '50s and '60s the news media took over the criminal trials in the name of the First Amendments Right of Freedom of the Press. However, it was carried too far, with cameramen crammed into every corner of the courtroom, snapping photos of defendants, attorneys, witnesses, and even jurors.

The legal community recognized the dignity of the court had been violated, so the law was changed to eliminate cameras in the courtroom except in certain controlled situations. The DA's office had received pressure from the media to permit cameras in the courtroom. As stated earlier, this issue was hotly debated in the criminal justice community. Elected DAs wanted to appease the media, while some of the trial prosecutors recognized the adverse effects of cameras in the courtroom, especially on the witnesses and the defense attorneys.

These litigators were warning the judges of the devastating negative effect that would occur ten years later in the O.J. Simpson trial. In that case, the news media turned the trial into a circus-like atmosphere. In the Joe Hunt case, the DA's Office agreed to TV coverage, but the trial prosecutor could object to certain witnesses being televised. Fred Wapner, the prosecutor, knew he could live with this type of negotiated agreement. In the Joe Hunt case, the DA's case revolved around Dean Kelly's testimony. Fred Wapner had gotten Dean into a Witness Protection Program, but if his face were televised he could be recognized and be threatened by anyone who watched television.

Another issue that had to be resolved was whether to try both the Joe Hunt and Jim Powell cases together. It is always beneficial to try co-defendants cases jointly. It certainly saves precious court time and is beneficial for the prosecution, in that their witnesses only have to testify one time. However, this is where the issue of bail changes the speed of a trial. Joe Hunt had a girlfriend, whose father was willing to put up his Bel Air mansion as security for the $2 million bail. Unfortunately, Powell didn't have a girlfriend whose father had a mansion, so Powell remained in jail because he couldn't raise bail.

Joe Hunt wanted his case continued forever since he didn't care if the case ever went to trial. Powell, on the other hand, wanted a speedy trial, and as a result the two cases were severed, allowing Powell's case to be tried first. This was highly advantageous to Joe Hunt since Dean Kelly would have to testify in the Powell trial first. So Joe had a transcript of Kelly's testimony, which could be used to impeach him on any inconsistencies that might occur in his testimony.

Most likely the biggest issue that had to be resolved before trial was the question of what, if any, mention could be made about the other murder case in San Mateo County. The DA's Offices in the two counties agreed they would separately try the murders that occurred in their jurisdiction. In other words, Ron Levin's murder case would be tried in Los Angeles County. The murder trial of Hedayat Eslaminia was still awaiting trial up north. Since no one had been convicted of that crime, it couldn't be revealed in the present case.

Nonetheless, the defense wanted to cross-examine Dean Kelly about his immunity agreement on the Eslaminia case. This created a difficult situation since the defense wanted to attack Dean's credibility but didn't want the jury to know about Joe's involvement in that case. The judge agreed the prosecution could mention all the parties who were charged in the other murder case. However, the judge admonished the prosecutor not to go into any of the details. The bottom line was the jury would learn that the defendant, Joe Hunt, was charged with another murder, but would not know what role he played in it.

The Defense raised another major objection that occurs in murder cases where a body has yet to be recovered. One of the common law rules is that an accused cannot be found guilty of murder unless there is a dead body. The rule came about because some accused persons were executed based solely on the fact that someone was missing. However, later the victim showed up, alive and well. This made it hard to undo an execution of the accused so a new law was created that required the Proof of Corpus Delicti. Basically, the prosecution must show the victim is dead, separate from the accused's statement that he killed the victim. Unfortunately, if a killer was good at disposing of a victim's body, then they were able to get away with murder.

Since Ron Levin's body was never found, the prosecution had a Corpus Delicti issue to deal with. Yet the law didn't like murderers getting off on a technicality. Therefore, an exception was created. If there was a mere scintilla of evidence that there was a 'criminal agency' such as the victim had been killed, that would be sufficient. The prosecution couldn't use Joe's statements alone that he had made to Dean Kelly or to the group of BBC members. But what the prosecution could use to prove the so-called "criminal agency" was the seven pages of the "To Do List." The court accepted that as a scintilla of evidence that a person was indeed killed.

Just as the pretrial motions were being resolved, out of the blue came the claim that the prosecution's star witness was being investigated for a murder. In October 1986, the body of a Richard Meyer was found in the Hollyland Motel. Allegedly a credit card receipt in the name of Dean Kelly was found in the motel room. The DA notified the Defense of the investigation. By December, Dean had been eliminated as a suspect. The Defense wanted to know the details of Dean's involvement. Fortunately, as much as Joe tried to have Dean connected to the murder, it turned out that Dean had a solid alibi. The matter was set for hearing, but suddenly it was abandoned by the Defense, without any reason stated.

Information was somehow obtained that Joe Hunt was trying to get to Dean Kelly to dissuade him from testifying. One of the more remarkable motions was the Defense trying to get the California State Bar to release their files on Dean Kelly. He had gone to Whittier Law School, where he graduated. Afterwards, Dean took the Bar Exam and passed it. He had applied to the State Bar for a license to practice law in California.

Joe Hunt tried to gain access to Dean's background investigation. The judge had an 'in camera hearing' with only the representative of records from the State Bar.

The judge reviewed the State Bar files and found nothing that could be used by the Defense to show that Dean wasn't a credible person. The Defense was on a fishing expedition, hoping to find some dirt on Dean to prevent him from testifying or to try to cast some doubt on his credibility.

CHAPTER 19 JURY SELECTION

Judge Laurence Rittenband was well known to the public since he had been a judge assigned to the Santa Monica Courthouse for many years. That judicial district included all the cases occurring from Beverly Hills, the Hollywood Hills, and all the way to the Pacific Ocean, including Malibu. This area was home to many movie stars and celebrities as well as the playground where they often got into trouble. Judge Rittenband had handled numerous publicity cases and he had grown fond of all the attention these cases created.

In1978, Judge Rittenband was the center of a media blitz when he presided over the scandalous Roman Polanski case. The public became acquainted with Polanski when his wife was viciously murdered by the Manson family members in 1969. Fortunately for Polanski, he was in Europe at the time of the brutal murders. Eight years later, Polanski used Jack Nicolson's house on Mulholland Drive to do a Vogue photo shoot involving a 13-year-old girl. No one else was present in the hilltop house except for those two. Polanski plied the girl with Quaaludes and champagne as they both sat naked in the Jacuzzi. He asked her if she was on the pill and she said, "No." Then he said it was okay and sodomized her in the master bedroom. Other salacious sexual acts were engaged in, and at the end of the photo shoot he cautioned her not to say a word to anyone.

The young girl's mother found out what had occurred and the police were called in to conduct an investigation. Ultimately, felony charges were filed for Rape by drugs, supplying drugs to a minor, Sodomy, and Oral Copulation. Incredible pressure was put on the young girl's family. They told the DA's Office they adamantly didn't want their 13-year-old daughter to testify in court. At the same time, Polanski didn't want the world to know how he had taken advantage of this young girl, especially sexually engaging her in such erotic acts.

Both sides, the DA's and Polanski's attorney, tried to figure out a plea bargain that they could agree to. It was negotiated that Polanski could plead guilty to 'Unlawful Sex with a Minor' and at time of his sentencing the other felony charges would be dismissed. All Polanski had to do was turn himself into the State Prison in Chino for a **90-day** Diagnostic Study. After the study was completed, the court would then determine the final sentence, which most likely would be straight probation.

Judge Rittenband had agreed to the terms of the plea bargain. For whatever reason, Polanski served only **47 days** at the Chino State Prison facility instead of the **90 days**. When Judge Rittenband found out, he was furious, since to him 90 days meant 90 days. There was some discussion in the judge's chambers that the judge was considering giving Polanski a state prison sentence with deportation after he had served his time. Somehow, Polanski received word that he might be going to state prison. In short order, he was on the next plane to Europe, where he remains to this day. Many attempts have been made to return him back to the USA, but all have failed. Throughout all the turmoil, Judge Rittenband seemed to enjoy the notoriety the Polanski case had brought to his courtroom.

On November 13, 1986, jury selection in the Joe Hunt case began and a large number of potential jurors were brought into Judge Rittenband's courtroom. In 1979, the California Supreme Court in ***Hovey vs. Superior Court*** had ruled trial jurors in capital cases are to be **questioned individually**. The court ruled, "... in future capital cases that portion of the voir dire of each prospective juror which deal with issues which involve death-qualifying, the questioning should be done individually and in sequestration." That new requirement lengthened the jury selection process since each juror had to be questioned outside the presence of the other jurors. During this time period, the high courts were striving for ***"Perfect Justice."*** Although the court was trying to help the Defense attorneys, in reality the process provided the prosecution with a slight advantage. Since the prosecution has to convince all 12 jurors, it was highly beneficial for the prosecutor to have the opportunity to ask more probing questions. In this way, the prosecutors gain an advantage in finding out who might be the holdout type or the contrarian type that could possibly result in a hung jury. (Later the law was changed to do away with individual questioning of potential jurors).

The big question for both sides was whether to have more men than women. Joe Hunt was a handsome, charismatic type who would appeal to women, especially young women. All indications were that the defendant would definitely be testifying. The prevailing view was that the prosecution would do better with male jurors. However, there was an opposing school of thought that women would be more introspective and see through Joe Hunt's sham of his 'Paradoxical Philosophy.' In the end, the gender ratio of the jury was ten women to two men. However, one of the men who didn't follow the judge's admonition to not read about the case in the newspaper was later removed from the panel. This meant that ultimately the jury was made up of eleven females. Many court observers thought it was a big mistake for the DA to gamble with so many women on the jury.

The jurors who were finally selected seemed to be congenial. The women jurors decided to exchange recipes. So every week one of the jurors brought in copies of their 'Recipe of the Week,' which were distributed to all the other jurors. However, one of the women became a little more creative and submitted the following recipe: "Stir Fried Inverted Butterflies (Also known as Mu Shu Porkbellies or Commodity Chop Suey) and is prepared as follows:

1. Invert a butterfly in frying pan.
2. Add some diced porkbellies and swiss frankfurters.
3. Simmer over a low heat for 10 minutes
4. A little margin may be called for to prevent shrinkage.
5. One can Hunt's tomato sauce and generous amounts of spice.
6. Simmer over low heat for an additional hour.

This dish may be served over rice, over noodles, or over the counter. It is best prepared ahead of time—it is a futures dish. Serves 4-6 financially secure people who wish to gain. (Low in calories and nutritional value—it is not advised for people with a faint heart condition)."

All the jurors had a chuckle with that week's recipe. This was a private matter that only involved the jurors. The Judge and attorneys were not aware of the 'Recipe of the Week.' However, when the male juror was excused for reading the news articles of the case, he gave the Defense attorney the above recipe. Not much was made of this 'Recipe of the Week' until the time of the appeal. Then, Joe Hunt made it the basis of one of the grounds to reverse the case for juror misconduct.

The appellate court stated, "We agree with the trial court's analysis of the recipe. While it satirized some of the evidence in the case, it didn't reflect a bias against the defendant. Not all types of misconduct carry the same risk of prejudice or compel an imputation of actual bias.

The recipe was not the type of a matter which is inherently prejudicial and its circulation among the jurors did not expose them to information that was not part of the trial record." In other words, Joe Hunt's conviction wasn't reversed, on the basis of the juror's creativity in her "Recipe of the Week".

CHAPTER 20 KELLY'S TESTIMONY

On January 15, 1987, the jury had been sworn in and they were all in their proper seats, eagerly waiting to listen to the attorney's explain what this case was all about. Judge Rittenband asked the Prosecutor, Fred Wapner, if he was ready to give his Opening Statement, to which he replied, "Yes, your Honor." He took a few steps from his seat at the counsel table, walked over to the lectern, and firmly placed his notes in order. Fred didn't waste any time explaining the motive for the killing. Joe Hunt wanted to get back at Ron Levin, who had played him for a fool. Then Fred indicated he would be using one of the BBC members, Dean Kelly, who was the closest one to the defendant who could relate how the actual murder was planned and carried out. He would tell how Joe Hunt, in his own words, described to him how he and Jim Powell shot and killed Ron Levin.

Fred didn't want to get bogged down in the tedious details, because this could distract the jurors. The prosecutor knew that his challenge with this jury was trying to persuade them that this handsome defendant, impeccably well dressed in a designer suit, could be capable of murder. Fred eased his way into revealing the seven-paged "To Do "List." He had a poster size blow up of the first page of the list.

He started with the title "AT LEVIN TO DO." Then he went down, line by line, stating each item, starting with "1. Tape Mouth," next line "2. Handcuff," and so on down the list. The jurors' eyes were bulging out trying to comprehend who in the world could be that methodical in preparing a checklist for murder.

Fred knew the defendant's attorney would try to explain away the list as a mere prank. Therefore, the prosecution wanted to sear this list into the memory of each one of the jurors. Fred wanted the jurors to have no doubt that the defendant, Joe Hunt, actually wrote this list. He explained it would be stipulated that it was Joe Hunt's handwriting, as well as that the thumbprint on the back of the paper was Joe's. The jurors were fixated on each line. Fred went on to say, "Why would the defendant make such a detailed list except for the very reason he didn't want any gaffes or slip-ups when committing the "Perfect Murder"?

To show how certain the prosecution was that Joe would testify, Fred spent part of his Opening relating the many reasons why the jurors shouldn't believe Joe. The prosecution said the witnesses would testify to all the shams and frauds Joe Hunt had committed on investors.

Fred also wanted to plant a seed that if Joe Hunt really wanted to find Ron Levin, why hadn't he spent time and money trying to track him down? The DA said the only resources spent looking for Ron Levin came from law enforcement.

Then it was the Defense's turn to give an Opening Statement. The lead Defense Attorney, Arthur Barens, promised Joe would take the witness stand and be able to explain everything. Also, they had a witness who would testify to seeing Ron Levin sign the Microgenesis agreement in Joe's office, the day before his disappearance. They were going to call witnesses who knew that Ron was about to be convicted of bankruptcy fraud. Also, witnesses would testify Ron Levin had his bail reduced so his parents wouldn't lose their house if he skipped out on the bail bond.

Barens knew he had to take on directly the "To Do List" and spin it so the jurors would lose sight of it. He indicated his client would explain it was a list to get even with Ron Levin for setting him up to look like a fool. He claimed it was something Joe had written out in his office. Then he said someone took it from Joe's office and gave it to Mr. Levin for him to claim to find it in Ron's house. To arrive at the conclusion Joe had nothing to do with the list getting inside Ron Levin's house was a mighty big stretch.

The "To Do List" had been mentioned by both sides, so the judge had copies made and handed them out to the jurors so they could refer to it when the various witnesses discussed it.

The time had come for the witnesses to appear in court and tell their story of what happened. The star witness for the prosecution was Dean Kelly. As Kelly walked up to the witness stand, Joe stared at him every step of the way. If looks could kill, Kelly would certainly have been vaporized into ashes. Since he had been the closest friend to the defendant, he was able to testify to so many of the facts regarding the case. He was used to set the stage as to Joe Hunt's background and in creating the Billionaire Boys Club. He related the conversations Joe had in his dealings with Ron Levin. He also testified that several days before the shooting, Powell had gone into Joe's office and someone fired a gun, making a popping sound. After everyone had left, Kelly entered Joe's office when it was empty. That was when he saw a handgun with a silencer attached to it, resting on Joe's desk.

In order to prove the murder, the prosecutor asked Dean about a meeting held on June 24, in which Joe told his most trusted members that he and Jim Powell had killed Ron Levin. The jurors were listening and taking notes when Kelly described how Joe explained the need to kill Levin in order to save the BBC. The defendant made it sound like a mere business decision to gain capital so the BBC could be refinanced. Since Kelly had numerous conversations with Joe, he was able to relate how Joe had taken dinner over to Ron Levin's house and had arranged for Jim Powell to come in and demand money. Powell pointed a gun at both of them, claiming Joe owed the Mafia money and could be paid from the money that Ron Levin owed Joe.

Dean Kelly further explained they got Ron to write a check for $1½ million on one of his Swiss bank accounts. After procuring the check, they took Levin into the bedroom, where Joe gave the cue and Powell shot Levin in the back of the head. Dean went on to say that Joe and Powell took Levin's body to Soledad Canyon to dispose of it. Then Joe described to Dean how they had used a shotgun to blow off parts of Levin's body so he couldn't be identified if his body was ever found. If that wasn't enough for the jury to digest, Dean went on to describe what surprised him the most, which was that Joe said he found it fascinating when they shot the back of Ron's head how his brain blew out and landed on the his chest.

By this time, some of the jurors looked a little pale, as though they had heard more than they wanted to know. The prosecutor, Fred, knew this case would be won or lost depending on how the jurors evaluated Dean's testimony. Fred knew the Defense was waiting to conduct their cross-examination. They were going to paint a picture of Dean being given complete immunity; therefore, he was willing to say anything to make the prosecution happy. Since Dean wasn't directly involved in Ron Levin's murder, the Defense couldn't attack the immunity agreement. However, the DA's Office had agreed to give him immunity in the Hedayat Eslaminia killing, in which he had been a direct participant. Fred was given the opportunity to bring out that Joe Hunt was also charged with that murder, even though the details could not be explained to this Santa Monica jury.

While Kelly was testifying, Joe was constantly scribbling notes, which he constantly handed to his attorney. Joe was very much involved in supplying questions to his attorney in hopes to trip up his old buddy Dean. Few witnesses have ever been subjected to such scrutiny on cross-examination as Dean. Throughout it all, Dean kept his composure and was very articulate in describing the activities of the BBC and Joe's involvement in the Ron Levin murder.

CHAPTER 21 OTHER PROSECUTION WITNESSES

The prosecution continued to call witnesses, including the two Robinson brothers. They were able to fill in some of the gaps relating to Joe's contact with many of the BBC members through the years, since they had all attended the Harvard Prep School together. Tom Robinson had known Joe for most of his life. The brothers said that Joe was a great debater who was very effective in persuading listeners. They were able to explain how Joe had come up with his 'Paradoxical Philosophy.' When they were cross-examined, the Defense tried to show the brothers had an interest in the case because they were involved in creating a TV mini-series about the Billionaire Boys Club.

Mr. Burns, inventor of the Cyclotron, was called on to explain the Cyclotron investment, which had faltered along the way. He explained how the BBC had hopes of selling these machines but there had been some technical difficulties that held up production. He also claimed someone had a judgment against Joe and those attorneys were tracking down the Cyclotron business in Arizona in order to collect on their judgment.

The prosecution called Mrs. Levin, Ron's mother, to state that she had not heard from her son since his disappearance on June 6, 1984. Ron was always in contact with his parents, even when he was traveling. The prosecution presented evidence from several financial institutions with accounts in Ron's name showing that there had been no activity such as any withdrawals or deposits. The only activity was the accumulation of monthly interest earned. This further showed Ron Levin's life patterns had completely ended on June 6, 1984.

Ron's father, Mr. Martin Levin, also testified that he had found a "To Do List." On cross-examination, the Defense tried to make an issue of the fact that Mr. Levin did not immediately turn over the list to the police.

They tried to paint a picture that evidence was being planted on the defendant, Joe Hunt. However, there was no connection as to why and how the "To Do List" would be given by some unknown person to Levin's parents.

There were over 50 witnesses brought in to spell out the actions of Joe Hunt and Jim Powell. Several witnesses came all the way from New York to explain how Jim Powell had tried to impersonate Ron Levin and tried to use his credit cards. Others testified about the Swiss bank account having a balance of only $49.

Other witnesses testified the BBC was a Ponzi scheme that couldn't generate sufficient funds to pay for expenses, which were running $70,000 per month. The prosecution was able to have witnesses identify Jim Powell, who earlier had been brought into court so everyone could see who they were referring to. One witness was the officer who had arrested Powell and had found a few 'Hit Man' books in the black bag he carried. When they searched Powell's place, they found several weapons, including a pistol, a derringer, a small black automatic, a pen gun, and a .357 caliber handgun.

The prosecution, with all their witnesses, had made their case and now it was time for the Defense to start presenting evidence of the Ron Levin "Sightings." Two people in September of 1986 believed they saw Levin at a gas station in Tucson, Arizona. They described him as having blue-gray eyes and about six feet tall. He was with a younger man and both were described as homosexuals. Two months later, a woman was reading Esquire magazine and saw a sketch of Ron Levin in a story about the BBC. She thought she recognized the sketch and read the description in the article.

When that woman was shown a photo lineup, she sort of picked out Levin's photo. When they used a photo of Levin without the beard the woman said she was 99% sure she and her friend had seen Ron Levin.

The Defense called Brooke Rogers (pseudonym), Joe's girlfriend at the time, to establish an alibi for him at the time of the murder. She said they had gone to a movie together. On cross-examination she was asked why she didn't tell police the defendant had an alibi. Why did she wait all these years to say that Joe was with her at the time of the murder? She became hostile toward the prosecutor when he tried to pin her down as to the time and place they went to the movies. He even said sarcastically, "If I give you some more time can you make something else up"? She was trying so hard to help her boyfriend but was not making a very convincing witness. Brooke's mother, Lynn Rogers (pseudonym), was also called as a witness for the Defense and also tried to be helpful, but she wasn't that convincing either.

The Defense continued to call witnesses to prove Levin did have a number of accounts that appeared to contain money. When Levin's executor took the witness stand, he stated that he hadn't been successful in finding any funds.

The expectation was high in the courtroom that Joe would charm the jurors with all of his answers. Then, out of the blue, the Defense attorney said, "The Defense Rests." The prosecutor, the news media, and the spectators were shocked that this young man, who could persuade the Rich and Famous to give him money to invest for them, didn't feel confident enough to testify. Many people were disappointed and felt deprived of an opportunity to watch the guru of the Billionaire Boys Club take the stage and prove his 'Paradoxical Philosophy' was true, in that, black is white and white is black, as well as good is the same as evil.

On Rebuttal, the prosecution wanted the jurors to know that the Tucson sighting was a fraud or a mere mistake. Detective Edmonds was called to the stand to state that he had gone to the service station in Tucson, Arizona, where Ron was supposed to have been seen. He testified that no one there could remember ever seeing him or anyone who looked like him. Det. Edmonds checked with the local police and they came up a with similar looking older, tall man with gray hair who lived in Tucson but had never been to L.A. They took a picture of him and showed it to the woman, who swore she had seen him. She claimed that person looked similar but it wasn't the one who she saw at the service station. This young woman claimed that the photo of Ron Levin was the most similar of all the photos she had been shown. Could she just be mistaken, or did she just want her 15 seconds of fame by testifying on live TV?

After four months of testimony, the trial came to an end. Fred, the prosecutor, gave a methodical Argument that showed how desperate Joe was and that he needed money fast. He concocted this plan to force Ron Levin to hand over funds he could use to save his BBC. Then the Defense surprised everyone by not having Joe Hunt tell his story. Sometimes that is the best Defense, merely claiming the prosecution didn't prove their case beyond a reasonable doubt. The Prosecution had heavily relied on Kelly and the "To Do List" to make their case. If the jury believed them, then they would be in good shape.

One of the points Fred alluded to was the fact the Defense didn't travel to Tucson to look for Ron Levin. If Joe Hunt was truly innocent, he would have gone to Tucson and totally explored the sighting. In this case, the Defense didn't do any follow-up investigation. This became a major issue in a later case named the O. J. Simpson case. In that later case, the defendant claimed someone else had killed his wife. As much as O.J. claimed someone else did it, he never spent any of his money looking for the killer. (He may have known a glance in a mirror would reveal the killer.)

CHAPTER 22 CONVICTION, PENALTY AND SENTENCE

After the judge had read the jury instructions, the jurors left the courtroom to commence their deliberations. At that time, the composition of the jury was made up of 11 women and one male. On April 22, 1987, after two and half days of deliberation, the jury buzzed, indicating they had reached a verdict. This came as a surprise to both sides since there were so many issues to be decided. Just months before, in the Jim Powell jury trial, the jurors deliberated for days, and even then they couldn't reach a verdict and a hung jury was declared.

In Judge Rittenband's courtroom, after everyone was in their place, the courtroom clerk read the verdict of Guilty of Murder in the first degree, as well as Special Circumstance of Murder during a Robbery. The judge gave the jurors two weeks off before they needed to start the Death Penalty phase of the case. The judge told Joe since he was convicted of murder his bail was revoked and he was committed to custody until the penalty phase of his case.

After the verdict, Joe Hunt made a comment to a news reporter. He predicted Levin would show up in a couple of years. He said, "It's just astonishing. It's a tragedy because Ron Levin is alive and I'm sure he will be found." Joe went on to say, "My memory has always served me and it certainly serves me now. Ron Levin is alive and this is one of those unfortunate circumstances of compounded effort. My own responsibility is to keep my chin up. That's the best that I can do."

The right to freedom in the life of the enigmatic Joe Hunt had come to an end in a most unceremonious act. The bailiff told Joe to empty his pockets and to take off his tie. Joe, in a matter-of-fact way, handed his personal items to his sobbing girlfriend. He gently leaned over and kissed her hand as she turned and ran crying out of the courtroom. Joe then turned and walked to the custody door of the courtroom. One of the bailiffs unlocked the door, and Joe walked into the custody holding area. At that exact moment, Joseph Gamsky Hunt would never walk the face of the earth again as a free man.

Several weeks later, the Penalty phase of the case began, with the same jurors, and both sides presented additional evidence. The prosecution can present any evidence as to Aggravating factors and the Defense can present evidence of any Mitigating factors. If the Aggravating factors substantially outweigh the Mitigating factors, then the sentence is set at Death; otherwise, the sentence is Life Without the Possibility of Parole. (LWOP)

The prosecution put on more witnesses to explain Joe's involvement in the death of Hedayat Eslaminia. They testified how he had planned and coordinated the kidnapping of Hedayat. Their testimony revealed how much suffering the victim went through before he suffocated to death. It would seem to be an Aggravating factor when a person, less than three weeks after killing Ron Levin, plans and carries out a similar scheme to get money out of Swiss bank accounts which resulted in the killing of another victim. The prosecution tried to prove Joe showed no remorse for taking these victims' lives. He had no sense of morality and believed he had done nothing wrong. On the other hand, Joe Hunt projected the image of a 25-year-old bright kid who had twisted values. Some might think, here is a young man who, with some help, could be rehabilitated.

As egregious as Joe's cold-blooded killings were, when those murders are compared to other murders, they may not be thought to be that aggravating. Joe Hunt, when compared to other murderers, might not be considered quite as evil when likened to Charles Manson (directed the brutal killing of at least six victims); Lawrence Bittaker (brutal killer of six young girls); Richard Ramirez (Night Stalker, brutal killer of more than 16 victims); Doug Clark (Sunset Slayer-Torturous Killer of six young girls); William Bonin (Freeway Slayer Killer of 12 boys); and the list goes on and on. Every Defense attorney wants their client compared to the most abominable killer in history. When jurors go down that path, it is understandable why it makes killers like Joe Hunt appear to be less malicious compared to the others. That may be the reason this jury, made up of 11 women plus the one male, decided to give Joe Hunt the benefit of the doubt and recommended a sentence of **Life Without the Possibility of Parole.**

CHAPTER 23 THE 60 MINUTES INTERVIEW

Sometimes strange cases even get stranger. As soon as Joe entered the gates of the State Prison, he started working on his appeal. He did an interview with Ed Bradley from the TV show "60 Minutes." He was very talkative in front of the TV cameras. He was asked about the "To Do List"—every listener was curious to know how he was going to spin that one. At trial, his Defense attorney had tried to imply that Mr. Levin, Ron's father, may have had something to do with planting it in his son's house. When asked by Ed Bradley, Joe admitted he wrote it but it was only meant to scare Ron into doing business with him. The list had nothing to do with the killing of Ron Levin.

People continued to come out of the woodwork claiming sightings of Ron Levin, to which the Defense would say, "I told you so." Joe wanted another trial since people had claimed to have seen Ron Levin in various parts of the world. At times the prosecution wondered if someone had cloned Ron Levin, since he seemed to show up at various places around the world. Joe made it sound like Ron was running from the law, yet he was continually being spotted.

Even a reporter from the City News Service claimed he had seen Ron Levin alive and well at some point. There had been several alleged Ron Levin sightings, but none of the look-a-likes were ever traced back to a certain person. They all seemed to disappear into thin air. One could describe it as 'Smoke and Mirrors,' which Joe was master at manipulating as he did in his business dealings.

There seemed to be an insatiable interest in Rich Kid Killers. As a result of the fascinating character of Joe Hunt, many books and magazine articles have been written about the Billionaire Boys Club. The legacy continues due to a mini-series that was fashioned after John Hunt's life story.

CHAPTER 24 TV MINI-SERIES

The Billionaire Boys Club became a cult story and was spun into a TV mini-series that had a major following. The TV writers wanted to give the series a flavor of the '80s with all its excessiveness. They presented the story by showing the various members who had testified in court. Each witness added something to the story. It was like putting a jigsaw puzzle together— piece by piece. The series depicted Joe Hunt as a distinctive character, supremely confident and a gifted liar. He truly saw nothing wrong taking the extra step to actually murder someone in order to obtain what he wanted. Even though the TV viewers of the mini-series knew the fate of Joe wasn't good, they were still captivated by him, just like all of his followers had been. Because the mini-series was so well written, it was nominated for an Emmy award. The popularity of the show appealed to a large segment of the population.

On July 30, 1989, a young man living in Beverly Hills just happened to have his TV on when the mini-series came on. He found the title intriguing. Erik Menendez called his older brother, Lyle, to come into his room and watch this program with him. The two slouched down in the overstuffed sofa in the family room and started watching the program about the rich kids of Beverly Hills. They quickly recognized some of the characters, and those they didn't know they could identify with. They felt a peculiar closeness to this story. They could relate to the same concerns the BBC members had. What was weird was they had felt the same pressures and stresses of the guys in the BBC. Lyle and Erik understood the feeling of never being good enough to satisfy their parents' expectations.

The brothers could see the parallel between the Robinson brothers and themselves. Both came from very prosperous families living in Beverly Hills. Their families didn't think they would succeed because they weren't competitive enough. The Robinson brothers were lured into the BBC's philosophy by starting at the top and staying at the top. Their parents always harped on the need to work your way up in an organization or a company. Joe's selling point was he would start the members out as CEOs, or president of a company. Lyle Menendez could especially recognize the usefulness of Joe's 'Paradoxical Philosophy.'

Undoubtedly, Lyle felt he could follow Joe's tenets, but he was also smart enough to avoid the same pitfalls because there were no members who could turn on him. The mini-series planted seeds in the minds of the brothers on how to murder someone and get away with it. Lyle liked Joe's point that everyone was capable of committing murder, under the right conditions. Desperate situations require desperate measures.

The TV mini-series illustrated the desperate situation Joe Hunt had found himself in when he was trying to save his Billionaire Boys Club from a financial meltdown. For the Menendez Brothers, the desperate situation was from being written out of their parents' will, which would be their financial ruin. Neither Joe Hunt nor the Menendez Brothers wanted to get their money the old-fashioned way, by working for it. The Rich Kids of Beverly Hills wanted to get it the easy way, even if it meant killing a few people. Lyle wanted to plan the killings so they could commit the 'Perfect Murders.' But Erik was too impatient and wanted to get started immediately. They watched the second episode on July 31, and within 20 days carried out the most horrific murders the City of Beverly Hills had ever seen.

On the following graphics page can be seen several of the books written about the brothers. Also listed is the Billionaire Boys Club TV mini-series.

Graphic 6

JOE HUNT
BILLIONAIRE BOYS CLUB

Many Books written about BBC & Joe Hunt

Menendez Brothers watched TV Miniseries

They wanted to be like them

That's where they got their idea to murder

CHAPTER 25 MENENDEZ FAMILY'S HOUSE IN BEVERLY HILLS

In 1986, the Jose Menendez family moved to Beverly Hills from Calabasas, which is located in the west end of the San Fernando Valley. Their new home was not below the tracks like Ron Levin's but above Santa Monica Blvd in a real exclusive area. They paid a mere $4 million for the 23-room Mediterranean-style mansion on Elm Street. At one time this was the abode for celebrities like Elton John and at another time the home of the pop performer Prince. The house was situated two blocks from the Beverly Hills Hotel, where movie stars and dignitaries stay when they are in town. Their house represented the fact that they, as a family, were living in the area with the zip code 90210, which meant **they had made it to the very top**.

This little City of Beverly Hills is home to 34,000 residents. Over the years, the city has been home to Cary Grant, Kirk Douglas, Glenn Ford, Lauren Bacall, Frank Sinatra, Madonna, Elvis Presley, Lana Turner, Charlton Heston, Gregory Peck, Bing Crosby, Milton Berle, Ann Bancroft, Charles Chaplin, and almost anyone else who was famous.

Just one street has been the home to more movie stars than any other street, that being North ***Roxbury Drive*** in Beverly Hills. Famous stars who live or have lived on this street include Lionel Barrymore, Maureen O'Sullivan, Mia Farrow, Marlene Dietrich, Lucille Ball, Jack Benny, Diane Keaton, Rosemary Clooney, Gorge Gershwin, Ira Gershwin, and many more.

In the very early days of the city of Beverly Hills, the land was used for growing lima beans until developers decided to start building houses on large lots. In 1919, Douglas Fairbanks and Mary Pickford bought land to construct an oversize mansion, which was referred to as 'Pickfair.' The glamour of movie stars like Pickford and Fairbanks building estates along the foothills encouraged other movie stars and filmmakers to follow their example. By the 1920s and '30s, Beverly Hills had gained the recognition that it was the place to live for the Rich and Famous.

Jose Menendez had become a mover and shaker in the entertainment world as he became the CEO of LIVE Entertainment, a subsidiary of Carolco Productions. For Jose, living in Beverly Hills was like a dream come true for a poor Cuban immigrant who had come to America. Having an address on Elm Street in Beverly Hills, CA 90210 told the world that **Jose Menendez** was an important person to be respected.

CHAPTER 26 GETTING RID OF MOM AND DAD

The date of Sunday, August 20, 1989, is well remembered but **NOT** due to the fact that 51 Brits lost their lives on that particular day when they were cruising down the Thames River on a foggy evening in London and crashed into a barge, sinking their boat in less than 30 minutes. The accident was the biggest maritime disaster in modern English history. However, the **world does remember that on that date Jose and Kitty Menendez were** slaughtered by their sons, Lyle and Erik Menendez.

That Sunday started out as a lovely sunny morning in Beverly Hills as the two Menendez brothers played tennis in their backyard court. Their parents sat on their patio sipping coffee while perusing the Sunday newspaper. This Ozzie-and-Harriet family moment would not last the whole day through. After a tennis workout, the brothers decided to go shopping at the Beverly Center, since Lyle would be leaving the next day to return to Princeton. Jose was so pleased his oldest son was going to an Ivy League school, especially since he had never been able to attend such a prestigious college.

Erik also needed to go shopping so he could look fashionable when he started at UCLA in just a couple of days. His father wasn't happy with his choice of university because Jose didn't consider UCLA a tried-and-true Ivy League school. Erik could have enrolled at UC Berkeley, which Jose considered an Ivy League school on the West Coast. But Erik was being stubborn about going to UCLA since many of his friends were going there and he wanted to stay with his clique of friends.

The brothers spent the afternoon leisurely visiting countless stores with their friends. As the evening approached, there was a meeting of the minds that a group of them would go see

Licence to Kill, a new James Bond movie at the Westwood Fox Theatre. This was one of the old-time theaters where Hollywood premieres were held. As huge as the theater was, the ticket line was wrapped all the way around the block, so Erik's friends agreed to change their plans and go elsewhere. They drove over to Century Plaza Mall Theater, which was showing *Batman Returns* where the line was half the size as in Westwood. One of them stood in line and purchased the tickets for everyone else.

By the time the movie was over it was after 9:30 p.m., and the common complaint from all of them was they were hungry since they hadn't had dinner. Some thought about going to the 'Taste of L.A. Festival' in Santa Monica, just to sample all the different foods. Others thought it was too late for the festival and opted for the Cheesecake Factory Restaurant in Beverly Hills. The group decided to drive over to the restaurant. Erik mentioned to his brother, Lyle, that he had forgotten to pick up his fake ID so he could drink alcohol. They agreed Lyle would take Erik back home to get his other ID, then they would all meet shortly at the restaurant.

Leaving the Century City Mall, Lyle drove his red convertible Alfa Romeo eastbound on Santa Monica Blvd. Coincidentally, the two brothers were driving the same street that Joe Hunt and Jim Powell had driven five years earlier when they were trying to dispose of Ron Levin's body that was in the trunk of their BMW. As a matter of fact, the Menendez brothers weren't far from Ron Levin's house.

Lyle zoomed along Santa Monica Blvd. at a quick pace. As he neared the turnoff for his folks' place he could see to his right the sign 'Beverly Hills Police Department.' He turned left and jockeyed one street over to Elm Street. At this hour at night, the Beverly Hills streets were completely empty of traffic. As they proceeded northbound on Elm Street, they proceeded by the stately houses with their splendid, well-manicured lawns reflecting the affluence of the neighborhood. They continued on without thinking they were traveling on the street where the movie *Beverly Hills Cop* had been filmed.

Lyle arrived at their Mediterranean style mansion and pulled into the driveway. They had left the security gate open for their convenience. Since it was Sunday evening, the maid had the evening off, so their folks were home alone. Lyle drove into the motor court, pulled up next to the house, and parked. The brothers jumped out and opened the trunk of their car and removed two items. They walked around the side of the house, all the way to the rear.

They snuck in through a French door they had left unlocked. Without making any noise, they maneuvered their way through the den. As they moved closer to the family room, they could hear the sound of the TV and knew their parents would be there watching TV. Their dad liked to watch old James Bond movies over and over again. They could hear the sound from the movie, *The Spy Who Loved Me,* one of his favorites. Both brothers walked on their tip toes, in order not to disturb their parents. They entered the darkened family room, in which a huge swordfish was mounted above the double doors.

The lights were turned down, and they recognized their parents from the flicker of light from the TV. Their father was seated on the sofa with his feet propped up on the coffee table. Their mother was lying down on the sofa with her head in Jose's lap. From the position of their bodies, they both appeared to have dozed off. Lyle entered the family room first, as Erik followed slightly behind him.

Both brothers raised their shotguns, placing the stocks against their shoulders. Pointing the barrels directly at their parents, they gradually pulled back on the triggers. Then there was a thunderous roar as the shotgun pellets ripped gaping holes into their parents' bodies.

CHAPTER 27 WHO WAS JOSE MENENDEZ?

Back in the 1960s, Jose Menendez was a true hot-blooded Cuban and proud of it. His parents were well established in the Fulgencio Batista world of Cuba. The family lived well since Jose's father had a successful accounting firm and his mother had been an accomplished sports swimmer. Life for Jose's family couldn't have been better. Then, all of a sudden, the world changed when the Cuban Revolution, led by Fidel Castro, came into power. Property rights were changed and the new Communist approach was to take from the well-to-do and give to the poor. By 1960, everything in Havana was topsy-turvy and the Menendez family lost all the trappings of the good life.

It was decided that Jose, who was16 years old at the time, would proceed with relatives to the USA and find a new life as a refugee. They settled in Hazleton, Pennsylvania, hoping to find the American Dream. Life was extremely tough for Jose; he didn't have any money, and on top of that, he didn't speak English. There was no safety net to help him climb from the bottom up. Jose was one of those quiet kids in high school, watching and listening trying to figure everything out on his own. He became self-reliant and studied like no other student in order to master the English language. For Jose, it was like a crash course in learning everything his fellow students had already acquired over their 16 years of life.

The result of Jose's effort was he had a strong resolve and it reinforced him with a self-confidence that he could master anything he put his mind to. Even with his studious effort, by his senior year, he still didn't have an impressive resume like his classmates. When it was time to apply for admission to a college, he couldn't compete with those headed to the Ivy League schools. This lost opportunity would forever stay with him. The one thing that came naturally to Jose was swimming. He took after his mother, who had been a champion swimmer in Cuba. Because of his high school swimming record, he was able to qualify for a swimming scholarship to Southern Illinois University.

Jose tried to get as much as he could out of attending the campus in Carbondale, Illinois. It was there, in his freshman year, that he met a young lady by the name of Kitty Anderson, who was in her senior year. It was extraordinary how they hit it off since both were reserved and quiet. Kitty recognized the boundless ambition and energy Jose put into everything he did. Kitty's background was totally different from Jose. Her parents were shopkeepers and had made a comfortable living for her family.

Jose and Kitty became inseparable and seemed to complement each other. Kitty was majoring in Communication and thought about pursuing a career in producing and directing commercial radio and TV programs in New York City. After graduation, Kitty decided to stay in Illinois to be with Jose. Jose's parents had left Cuba and immigrated to New York City. Jose and Kitty decided to elope and were secretly married in 1963. Jose couldn't resist the urge to leave Southern Illinois for the Big Apple.

This was a major change for both of them. Kitty immediately found a job teaching in a grade school, which brought in money for both of them to live on. Jose enrolled in Queens College, City University of New York, where, in 1967 he received a business degree, and later earned his CPA. He left academia by taking an accounting position at Coopers & Lybrand, thereby starting his business career.

CHAPTER 28 JOSE'S CAREER

Jose projected a hard-working image and it didn't go unnoticed. A small company, Lyon Container, offered Jose the job as Controller of the company. Jose put his whole heart and soul into the job and managed to make the company profitable. Taking that position meant that Jose and Kitty had to move back to Illinois. It wasn't long before he was named president of the company. By the time Jose was 25 years old he had started the climb up the ladder of success. However, one of Jose's traits was to be forceful in making changes. It wasn't long before Jose was clashing with the chairman of the board as to the future of the company.

Jose was smart enough to know it was time to move on and found a new position with the Hertz Company. He became an executive in the car leasing division, requiring him to move his family again (this time it included his one son, Lyle) back to the East Coast to New Jersey. At that time, another guy from New Jersey, by the name of, Bruce Springsteen was getting started nearby. What's amazing is how the 'Bosses' songs ***Born in the USA*** and ***Born to Run*** exemplified Jose Menendez's drive to make it big in the USA, even though he hadn't been born in the USA.

It wasn't long before Jose ascended the corporate ladder to become the Chief Financial Officer. His ambition drove him even higher to become Hertz's worldwide general manager at the age of 35. Someone who had clawed his way to the top obviously ruffled some feathers and there were those who claimed he had abused some of his subordinates. It was hard to say whether all the claims were well founded or merely jealous colleagues who were left behind as Jose zipped past them.

The way Hertz handled this personnel clash was to transfer Jose over to its entertainment division, which included RCA Records. Jose had no background in the entertainment industry, and initially all he saw at RCA was overpaid and over-the-hill musicians who weren't producing any new hits. It wasn't rocket science that RCA needed new talent, so he signed on the Eurhythmics, a British duo consisting of Annie Lennox and David A. Stewart. Their album ***Sweet Dreams Are Made of This*** was a smash hit. Then Jose added to the RCA stable Jefferson Starship, a well-seasoned American rock band. They had a number of hits for RCA on their ***Modern Times*** album with its hit, ***Find Your Way Back***, and a later album, ***Winds of Change*** in 1982. By 1985, at the age of 41, Jose became the Executive Vice President and CEO for RCA Records, Worldwide Operations. Even with all the innovative ideas Jose incorporated into RCA, the company was never able to turn the business around and become a financial success.

By 1986, Jose could see his career had plateaued at RCA Records and started asking around for other job opportunities. He learned about an opening at L.I.V.E. Entertainment, a video-distribution and duplication company that had merged with a part of Carolco Pictures. It sounded promising, but the downside was the fact it was on the West Coast. The family had lived in Princeton, New Jersey, for 14 years. Kitty had finally found her dream house, a white Cape Cod house with a white picket fence around it. It was set on a wooded estate with a giant pond for a backyard. She loved it and had told her friends she was content to spend the rest of her life there.

Jose couldn't walk away from this opportunity to try and financially turn around L.I.V.E. Entertainment, which had lost $20 million in the past year. Jose's salary of

$1.3 million provided the incentive to transplant his wife Kitty and Erick to the Los Angeles area.

The following graphic page shows where the family lived in Princeton NJ. Also listed are the various jobs that Jose had on the East Coast.

Graphic 7

CHAPTER 29 BROTHERS GROWING

Lyle was born January 16, 1968, when the family was living in the New York area. And three and a half years later Erik was born on November 22, 1971, in New Jersey when Jose was working for Hertz. By that time, the family had moved near Princeton, New Jersey, where the boys were enrolled in a prestigious private school, Princeton Day School. The brothers were considered to be just average students. Their teachers suspected both brothers had some form of a learning disability, because Lyle had difficulty concentrating on his assignments and Erik seemed to have some education problems as well.

The brothers were highly protective of each other, but their personalities were actually dissimilar. Lyle was categorically the stronger personality and thought well of himself. Erik was almost the total opposite, seemingly meek, with extreme sensitivity. Jose wanted so desperately to make sure both boys would be able to reach the top without having to struggle like he had. From Jose's prospective, a child had to learn to be self-reliant in order to survive the unexpected challenges of life. As a result, Jose set up a rigid schedule for the boys to follow, since every minute of the day was to be spent educating and improving themselves.

A better part of each day was set aside for reading, in order to prepare them to be better students. The kids felt the pressure from their father and both developed a stuttering problem. This was followed by abnormal stomach pains and constant grinding of their teeth. Strangely, Lyle at the age of 14 had some emotional maturity problems, including bed wetting and playing with his stuffed animals. Neither brother embraced their dad's philosophy of working hard to be successful.

To endure the high expectations of their father, the boys turned to relying on each other for support. Both of them gravitated to sports, where they were able to excel. They didn't like team sports and felt most comfortable with the individual sport of tennis. Lyle's perseverance elevated him to the top-seeded tennis player at his school.

Lyle was not interested in going on to college. He told his friends he wanted to own a restaurant and felt the business experience would satisfy his father. He was wrong, and Jose demanded he enroll in an Ivy League school. In 1986, he applied to Princeton, where he was summarily rejected because of his mediocre grades in high school. He spent a year at a community college, and then reapplied to Princeton. His second application emphasized his tennis abilities and pointed out his ethnicity (Menendez being Hispanic). It is unknown whether the fact that his father had donated $50,000 to the university had any effect on his acceptance to Princeton.

Jose was ecstatic. He finally had a son attending an Ivy League school. However, as hard as Jose worked to get Lyle into Princeton, Lyle had other ideas. A young lady, named Jaime, came into Lyle's life. She was a waitress who was five years older than Lyle. Lyle announced he was in love with her and that he planned on marrying her, at his tender age of 19. Jose was furious after all the work he had to done to get Lyle accepted to Princeton. Jose went on and on that 19 was too young to get married.

What was counterproductive about his objection was that when he was 19, he wanted to marry Kitty and both of their families had objected.

Now his son was attempting to follow in his father's footsteps. Jose had to find a way to derail this marriage idea. Somehow, Jose persuaded Lyle's girlfriend to move to Alabama to teach tennis. This didn't solve the problem. Lyle, like a puppy dog, followed Jamie to Alabama. Jose realized this called for desperate measures, so he worked it out with a sponsor to have her relocated to Europe. Now Jose believed he had solved the problem with Jaime since she had moved all the way to Europe. What Jose didn't consider was his son's perseverance, because Lyle followed her to Europe.

With some threats and additional money, Jose persuaded Lyle to return to the States to start his freshman year at Princeton. Jose was pleased he could tell all his friends his son was enrolled in one of the top universities in the country.

Princeton is a school built on tradition, dating back to 1893, in which every freshman signs a letter promising to obey the honor code. This didn't concern Lyle since he knew his dad could take care of any problem he might get himself into.

During the first semester, Lyle had a laboratory assignment in Psychology 101 class. He had to turn in a homework assignment, which he hadn't done. So he copied his lab partner's notes and turned them in as his own. As the instructor was reviewing the students' papers, he noticed that Lyle's paper was identical to his partner's. In other words, he hadn't tried to disguise or make any effort at all to cover up his plagiarism. The instructor found the cheating to be so blatant that he reported it to the campus administrators.

Although this didn't seem to be a huge deal for Lyle, it was for the school. There was a four-hour hearing with the Disciplinary Committee, where it was decided to suspend Lyle for one year. When Jose found out about the suspension, he went on the offensive. He demanded to meet with the president of Princeton. Jose pleaded with the president that this was a minor mistake on a homework assignment and the punishment didn't fit the violation. Even with all of Jose's protesting, the president wouldn't revoke the suspension, but did indicate the school would give him another chance again next fall.

This confrontation didn't help Jose understand his son any better. Lyle pleaded with his dad to let him go to UCLA, but Jose wouldn't hear of it. He insisted Lyle had to attend an Ivy League school and UCLA didn't qualify. Now Lyle needed a place to live while waiting to get back into Princeton. By this time, Jose, Kitty, and Erik had moved to the West Coast, where Jose was the boss of LIVE Entertainment. Since Jose wanted to teach Lyle about his job, he gave him a position at the company examining expense reports and finding ways the company could be more efficient. Jose also wanted Lyle to be treated like any other employee. Lyle wasn't thrilled about the idea of working for any company, let alone his dad's. As the year progressed, Lyle would arrive late for work and some days, he totally failed to show up all. On nice days, he would end up playing tennis with his friends, something he enjoyed. Many of the other employees resented Lyle, who came across as arrogant and completely disinterested in his job.

Finally, some of the employees had enough of Lyle and one of the managers explained the situation to Jose. Jose's response to the manager was, what would you do if he was any other employee? The manager said he would fire him. Then Jose said, "Ok, then he's fired." That evening must have been an odd dinner after everyone was seated around the dinner table and the head of the house, the father, said to his eldest son, "What was your day like?" The son turned to his dad and said, "Well, I was fired by you, dad, for being a lousy worker."

Obviously, that dialogue didn't happen exactly that way, but Lyle was humiliated for being fired by his dad. Lyle thought his dad was supposed to be more protective and be there to bail him out of bad situations. This incident had a lasting impression on Lyle, in that it appeared his father had given up on him.

The following graphic page shows the Menendez family when they moved to Calabasas while Lyle remained at Princeton.

Graphic 8

MENENDEZ BROTHERS

When Jose got job at Carolco the family moved to Calabasas

Family Deep Sea Fishing

Lyle remained at Princeton

CHAPTER 30 ERIK

As previously mentioned, in 1986 the Menendez family moved to Calabasas, California, which is located on the west end of the San Fernando Valley. The area is made up of rolling hills with large ranch-style homes. Many of the haciendas still have horses on their spacious lots. The Menendez family found a large estate that contained a lighted tennis court adjacent to an enormous swimming pool. Calabasas is a small community of 23,000 with homes for the rich and famous, including Katherine Jackson and all of Michael's children; the Kardashians; Kris Jenner; Lady Gaga; Jennifer Lopez; Demi Moore; Will Smith and family; Britney Spears; Tori Spelling; LeAnn Rimes; Lisa Marie Presley; Miley Cyrus; Justin Bieber; and Cameron Diaz.

At that time, Calabasas had the dubious distinction of being the heart of the lucrative pornographic adult entertainment industry; however, as the internet matured, the porn business faded away. Erik had started as a sophomore at Calabasas High School and seemed to gravitate to the kids who were cocky, with a rebellious streak in them. Again, the area where Erik excelled was in his ability to play tennis. He applied himself and improved enough to be the number-one-ranked player on the team. Craig Curry (pseudonym) was the captain of the tennis team, so it was only natural that Erik and Craig became close friends.

Their relationship wasn't abnormal, but what resulted from it was uncanny. The two collaborated on a screenplay titled ***Friends,*** consisting of 62 pages. At the time, no one thought anything about it. But, several years later, it was like a blueprint to the fate of the Menendez family. The story was about a son, from an affluent family, who read his parents' will and from that learned he would inherit $157 million. Shortly thereafter, the son murders his parents in order to instantly receive his inheritance.

By the summer of 1988, Erik was spending more time with his brother Lyle, since he had been suspended from Princeton and their father had fired Lyle from his job for being lazy. This put the brothers in a problematic financial situation, since all the other kids in Calabasas had spending money they had either earned or were given by their family. Jose didn't believe in giving a 'free' allowance. He believed the boys had to earn any money they received. The boys loathed the type of jobs he would pay them to do

The brother's predicament was that they didn't have any spending money. They considered the various options available to them. They were aware that all their neighbors were exceedingly prosperous. The brothers' rationale was the only natural thing to do would be to steal from their new neighbors. Lyle with several of his friends snuck into a neighbor's house and took some items. They realized how easy it was to burglarize their neighbors. Erik joined in to prove he could steal just like his big brother. Thus began the wave of burglaries in the Calabasas neighborhood. The boys knew when their friends' houses would be empty, and they would climb in by a back window. Since they were familiar with the layout of the house, the two brothers could quickly find things of value. They could do burglaries quickly and without any notice since they didn't stand out in the area.

Jose would have been proud of his sons for being so efficient and effective in pulling off dozens of burglaries without raising any suspicion. Of course, Jose would never have contemplated his sons being professional burglars. So all summer long the Sheriff's Department was running around taking burglary reports, and they had no suspects. That was until a deputy Sheriff who was assigned to work traffic enforcement made a 'traffic stop' when Erik was driving his car. For whatever reason, the deputy became suspicious of items in the back of the car and asked for permission to look in the trunk. When Erik opened the trunk, it was full of VCRs, TVs, and all sorts of other stolen property.

Erik was busted, and his brother Lyle was implicated as well. They were connected to numerous burglaries with losses totaling over $100,000. When Jose found out what his sons were involved in, he was furious. Although Jose understood this could be a teaching moment for his sons, he also realized he had to find a way to come to their aid and contain the damage to the reputation of the family name. The first thing Jose did was find the best criminal defense attorney and see what could be done. He hired Jerry Chaleff, who had achieved notoriety when he tried the Hillside Strangler case. Chaleff was a good choice because he knew how the criminal justice system worked. Jose stressed he didn't want any son of his to serve any time in jail. The defense attorney asked Jose the ages of the two boys and was told that Lyle was 21 and Erik was still only 17 years old.

Chaleff saw his best bargaining chip was the fact that Erik would be treated as a juvenile because he was under the age of 18, which meant next to nothing would happen to him. He worked out a plea bargain with the DA in which Erik would admit to the burglaries if the charges against Lyle were dismissed. In other words, Erik would take the fall for both of them. The question was, what would the sentence be for Erik? It was agreed that Erik would get probation, which would include working with the homeless and undergoing psychological counseling, as well as good old dad would write a check for $11,000 to the victims to cover some of the stolen items that were not recovered.

One would think the two brothers would be ecstatic that their dad had come to their rescue and prevented them from serving any jail time, as well as saved their future. Lyle had his charges dismissed, and Erik could have his juvenile record sealed upon successfully completing probation. Life went on, without any thanks to Jose. All Jose got from all of this was the Calabasas neighbors now shunned the Menendez family. Their friends could see Erik running around town, not showing any remorse. As a result of the burglaries, the Menendez family received harassing calls and a chilly reception from their neighbors. It wasn't long before Jose realized it was time to move on. As Jose tells the story, they felt safer living in Beverly Hills, where no one knew about the burglaries.

CHAPTER 31 LIFE GOES ON

Jose's summer was consumed in trying to save his sons' reputations. When summer ended, Lyle packed up his bags and returned to Princeton. Things didn't proceed well when he arrived back at college. Unbelievably, Lyle had been assigned a roommate in his dormitory room. Lyle wasn't going to permit a stranger to room with him, so he threw the roommate's belongings into the hall. He told the dorm advisor he wanted a single room. Jose wrote a letter to the school staff, asking that Lyle be given a single room. Immediately, Lyle was assigned a single room.

In the early spring of 1989, Lyle met Donovan Guthman (pseudonym) at school. The two had a lot in common and became close friends. Jose and Kitty liked this friendship and felt Donovan was a good influence on Lyle. One of the benefits of having Donovan around was the fact he was willing to do Lyle's homework assignments, helping to keep Lyle from flunking out.

However, something unfortunate happened after Spring break in 1989. Some students were accusing Donovan of stealing from them. The strange thing was, Lyle didn't even come to Donovan's defense; instead, he joined the others in forcing him to quickly leave town. What was important about this fact was that Donovan left so quickly that he didn't take his wallet containing his California driver's license and Social Security card. Lyle, for whatever reason, picked up the wallet and threw it in with his personal belongings. This act of keeping Donovan's identification would later become crucial when the brothers decided to purchase two Mossberg shotguns at the Big Five Sporting Goods Store in San Diego.

CHAPTER 32 DIFFICULT TIMES

Jose's job at L.I.V.E. Entertainment was very demanding of his time and resulted in the business doing very well. The company executives were impressed with his achievements, so much so that the company went so far as to renegotiate Jose's contract until 1991, even adding in a life insurance policy. The company took out a $5 million policy for Jose's family; however, the papers hadn't been drawn up or signed as yet.

The Menendez family had its share of problems. Lyle wasn't a source of pride and joy for the family. First off, he was doing poorly academically and receiving "Fs" in most of his classes, even though his friend Donovan had earlier helped him with his assignments and papers. The Discipline Committee placed Lyle on academic probation. He told his dad it wasn't his fault. He told him they were coming after him because of a pool table that was damaged during a social event in the dorm recreation room. He claimed the Committee was personally attacking him.

Another form of bad news for Jose was that Lyle said his new girlfriend Christy, who was nine years older than him, announced to his parents that Christy was pregnant. Jose and Kitty didn't like Christy and thought she was out to get a rich husband. Jose met with Christy and somehow she ended up with $100,000 and had an abortion. Jose thought he was doing the best thing for his son.

That wasn't the only bad news from Lyle. Somehow, he had his New Jersey driver's license suspended for bad driving. However, that wasn't the end all of Lyle's bad driving. One night, after everyone had left the country club, Lyle and a friend took some golf carts for a spin around the clubhouse greens. As they raced from green to green, they did wheelies, tearing up the turf and causing considerable damage. The country club didn't take this vandalism lightly, and as a result, the Menendez family was not just suspended but also no longer welcome at this prestigious country club.

This was like the last straw that broke the camel's back for Jose. He was so humiliated in front of people he wanted to impress. Jose's reputation was suffering from the actions of his irresponsible, immature sons. Jose and Kitty didn't know how to get across to their sons that this foolhardiness had to end. It seemed nothing they said or did made any impression on them. Jose and Kitty wondered what could be the most extreme measure they could take. Because of Jose's new life insurance policy, he and Kitty had to decide who should be listed as their beneficiaries.

They thought maybe disowning the boys might grab their attention. They sat both of the boys down and told them they were taking their names out of their wills and would not be listing them as beneficiaries on their life insurance policy. They told the boys they would have to prove to their parents they had changed and deserved to be beneficiaries in their will. As they say in tennis, the ball was in the boys' court and now it was up to them. If they wanted the good life, they would have to change their ways. **How could such good intentions by their parents turn out to be so deadly?**

CHAPTER 33 DAYS LEADING UP

Jose and Kitty had given their sons an ultimatum. As parents, they were desperate to find the key to try and turn their kids around. Kitty knew Erik was still receiving therapy from Dr. Jerome Owens (pseudonym), who was the psychiatrist the court had appointed to consult with Erik during his probation for the burglaries. Part of that agreement was Kitty could talk to Erik's psychiatrist to learn what his problems were. It was never known exactly what Dr. Owens told her but, what is known is that Kitty immediately talked to her own therapist, saying her sons were narcissistic and sociopaths. It was inferred that Kitty had received that information from Dr. Owens.

The result of that information changed how Kitty responded to her sons. She took the house keys from both of the boys. In order for them to enter the house on Elm Street, they had to have their parents open the door to let them in. Even when the boys came home late, Kitty would come downstairs to unlock the front door. It is unknown what spurred Kitty to take such drastic measures at night. She even locked her bedroom door when she was sleeping. She also had an unloaded rifle standing up and ready in her bedroom closet.

Earlier, in August 1989, the brothers went to the Big 5 Sporting Goods Store in Santa Monica, in an attempt to purchase two shotguns. Did the sales person ask too many questions? Did the brothers get spooked based on the fact that they had to produce identification? For whatever reasons, they decided not to make the purchases locally. What is known is both brothers traveled two hours to San Diego, where they visited another Big 5 Sporting Goods Store. This time they had the identification from Donovan, which they used, to make the purchase of two Mossberg shotguns. They were pleased with themselves for pulling off the purchase using Lyle's old friend's name. How fortuitous it was that Lyle had the smarts to hang onto Donovan's wallet.

Now that the brothers had the instrumentality (the shotguns) ready, it was only a matter of finding the perfect time to commit the murders. The weekend of August 19 was the last time the family would be together, since Lyle would leave on Monday to return to Princeton to start the new school year. Erik was also leaving to start at UCLA in a few days. Jose was still upset at Erik for selecting UCLA, especially after he had received admission to UC Berkeley. UC Berkeley was considered the Ivy League school on the west coast; still, Erik would not consider going up to the San Francisco Bay Area to attend Berkeley. Jose was so concerned with image that anything short of an Ivy League university wasn't good enough for his sons.

On Saturday, August 19, 1989, Jose wanted the family to do something together so he arranged for them all to go on a 'deep-sea fishing trip.' Over the years, these fishing trips had been enjoyed by the entire family. When the boys were younger, they looked forward to going fishing. It was always very competitive to see who caught the biggest fish or the most fish. Jose was hopeful this fun event would re-cement the cracks in the family's relationship.

The fishing crew remembered the Menendez family well. They also recalled that they found the family slightly dysfunctional. Jose was doing some serious fishing at the rear of the boat and Kitty was downstairs in the captain's cabin struggling with sea sickness. What seemed so strange to the crew was that the two sons were up front on the bow of the boat talking to each other. The brothers didn't attempt to do any fishing. It was an evening of deep-sea fishing, where they were out from 4:00 p.m. to 11:00 p.m. During the entire time, the crew never saw any intermingling between the boys and their parents.

No matter how strained things had gotten, Jose was hopeful some type of family activity might magically ease tensions. As the boys were about to leave for college, their parents thought maybe they would gain some maturity. The deep-sea fishing trip didn't seem to be the vehicle to bring the family together. No one appeared to enjoy themselves, except possibly Jose, who was the only one who caught any fish. Most likely, the boys would have preferred spending the evening doing other things, like practicing with their two new shotguns or working on their alibis.

Exactly 24 hours after returning home from the deep-sea fishing trip, Lyle lifted the twelve-gauge Mossberg shotgun, aimed it at his father, then gently pulled the trigger as the shotgun resounded. He tilted the shotgun back in position and fired a second time, but this time the French windows were shattered. Erik became involved, shotgun firing his in the direction of Kitty, who had jumped up from the sofa. Then Lyle walked slowly behind his father and, from the back of the sofa, lifted the shotgun to the back of his father's head and squeezed the trigger, blowing Jose's brains out onto the sofa in front of him.

This moment of mayhem was similar to the actions of Joe Hunt who used a shotgun to blow Ron Levin's brains out onto his lap. But this pandemonium wasn't over yet, as the brothers continued to shoot at their mother. Kitty lost her balance and fell between the sofa and coffee table. Possibly she recognized the killers as her sons since she put her hands up, either to block her view of the shooters or to protect herself. As she staggered to rise up, one of her sons shot her again in the chest area. This shot was so close that the wadding from the shells penetrated her leg.

The brothers were perplexed as to how their mother kept crawling, trying to get up. They didn't know what to do with her, so they ran out to Lyle's car, reloaded the gun with birdshot, and returned to the family room. Then one of them took the shotgun, placed it against the cheek of Kitty's face, and pulled the trigger. This blast was so strong that it ripped off half of Kitty's face. At that point neither Jose nor Kitty was moving; nonetheless, their bloodied bodies continued to ooze blood onto the sofa and carpet.

By 11:00 p.m., the first part of the killing was complete, and now it was time to move on to step two, which was the cover-up phase.

On the following graphic page are photos and a diagram of the family room where the parents were shot.

Graphics 9

MENENDEZ FAMILY ROOM

Where Menendez Bros Shot their Parents who were on the Sofa

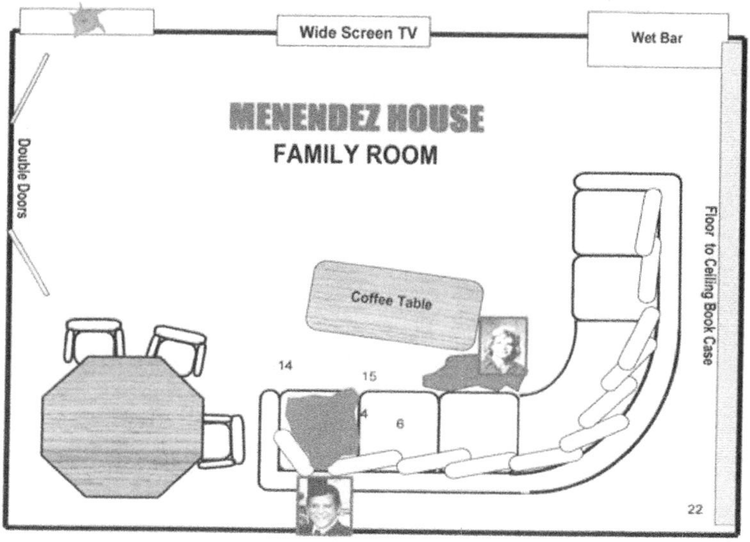

CHAPTER 34 AFTER THE SHOOTING

After pulling the triggers on the shotguns and watching their parents gasp their last breath, the brothers realized the killing of one's parents wasn't all that difficult to do. Yet, their real work was about to begin. First, they needed to take the shotguns and lock them up in Lyle's car, which was parked in the car court. The numerous shotgun blasts had been loud. Since it was a warm August evening, all the neighbors had their windows open. The boys believed that someone would call the police department, and they just waited for them to arrive.

They had set up their alibi by being with their friends and going to the movies at the Century City Theater. They would claim that they came home and found their parents had been shot in their family room. All was worked out and they remained waiting for the police to arrive. However, as the brothers sat on the stairs waiting, they couldn't hear any police sirens coming up the street. They wondered what went wrong and why hadn't a neighbor called about hearing loud gunshots. After a considerable time Kyle decided that he would call the police and report the fact that their parents had been shot to death. The call was made at 11:47 p.m. on August 20, 1989, to the Beverly Hills Police Department and is as follows:

Dispatcher: Beverly Hills Emergency

Lyle Menendez: Yes, police, uh...

Dispatcher: What's the problem?

Lyle: We're the sons... (*caller begins to cry)*

Dispatcher: What's the problem? What's the problem?

Lyle: (*Still crying*) They shot and killed my parents!

Dispatcher: What? Who? Are they still there?

Lyle: Yes

Dispatcher: The people who...

Lyle: No, no.

Dispatcher: They were shot?

Lyle: Erik, man, don't.

Dispatcher: (*Talking over the background sounds of screams and Lyle shouting, "Erik, Shut up!"*) I have a hysterical person on the phone. Is the person still there?

2nd Dispatcher: What happened? Have you been able to figure out what happened?

Lyle: I don't know.

2nd Dispatcher: You came home and found them shot?

Lyle: My mom and dad

Dispatcher: Are they still in the house, the people who did the shooting?

Lyle: (*Screaming)* Erik! Get away from them!

2nd Dispatcher: Who is the person who is shot?

Lyle: My mom and dad!

As discussed earlier, when Ron Levin's parents and friends contacted the Beverly Hills Police about a possible murder, there was first denial by the city officials. The reason was that those things just didn't happen in the CITY OF BEVERLY HILLS. Keep in mind, in most years, this upscale city didn't even have one homicide for many years. This can be seen with the first dispatcher calling in a second dispatcher because she couldn't believe a call coming in regarding two persons being shot.

Even though the dispatcher had doubts as to whether anyone could be murdered in Beverly Hills, she still dispatched a unit to respond to the Elm Street address. As the police arrived in this quiet area there was nothing amiss, only tranquility. The officers saw four vehicles in the front motor court area, directly in front of the house. A large Mercedes was parked adjacent to the front door, and another car was next to it. To the north side was a red Alfa Romeo convertible pulled perpendicular to the house and further over a smaller car. Nothing looked suspicious, and the officers had to wonder what type of hoax was being played on them?

The officer waited for backup, and when he arrived the two wondered what to do. The dispatcher indicated that two men were inside sitting on the stairs. One of the officers yelled for the men to come outside. They waited, looking at the front door when all of a sudden a young man came running out the door followed by another. Were these suspects or victims trying to get away from some type of shooter? They ran slightly past the officers and fell to their knees.

They were shouting, "Oh my God, I can't believe it!" The officers approached cautiously as they tried to get some information from them. One identified himself as Lyle Menendez and stated he and his brother had come home and found their parents shot to death in their family room. The younger man, who was identified as

Erik Menendez, was continually sobbing and acting irrational as he hit his head against one of the trees at the front of the mansion.

After one of the officers checked inside the house, he confirmed there were at least two dead bodies in what appeared to be a family room. The lead officer reached for his radio and notified the dispatcher that in fact there had been a double homicide. This was something that hadn't occurred in Beverly Hills for years. Needless to say, this event was going to light up the switchboard at the police department. The Chief of Police, Marvin Iannone, was contacted, and he immediately called Detective Les Zoeller and told him he was assigned the case. (Of course, you the reader already know about Det. Zoeller, since several years earlier he had conducted the investigation in the Joe Hunt case.)

CHAPTER 35 WHAT TYPE OF HOMICIDE?

Even though it was after midnight, Det. Zoeller reported to the Menendez mansion on Elm Street. He found the victims' bodies in the family room, where there was a definite appearance of an overkill. When commencing a homicide investigation, the detective starts the elimination process. First, could it have been a burglary in which the victims somehow surprised a burglar? This was immediately rejected because the victims appeared to have either been sitting or lying on the sofa, not in any position to surprise a burglar. Could it have been a 'cat burglar' who snuck in when the residents were asleep? There was no point of entry, such as door or window broken or ajar.

Next, Det. Zoeller considered whether it might have been a home invasion robbery. He checked out the various rooms but didn't find anything missing or any drawers that had been rummaged through. If this was a robbery, the victims' wallet or purse would have been taken or gone through. It seemed as if nothing was adding up.

As much as one doesn't want to think of a possible murder suicide, could the husband have killed the wife and then shot himself? Or vice versa? But the way the bodies had been shot numerous times quickly eliminated a murder-suicide theory. With there being no forced entry, the logical conclusion was the shooter had to have been let in or had a key to the house. It wasn't long before Det. Zoeller recognized this homicide wasn't going to be easily solved. At this time, all the detective could do was have the CSI team come in and try to do some magic in hopes it would uncover some clues.

Another detective had the brothers go to the Police Department, which was located several blocks down the street. There, Sgt. Thomas Edmonds interviewed them. Basically, he wanted to determine what they could tell him about what happened at the house or who might be behind the killings. Since the detective didn't consider the brothers to be suspects, they were interviewed together. The advantage of having the brothers in the interview room together was that Lyle could console Erik, his younger brother, who was sobbing uncontrollably. He seemed so distraught that he wasn't able to answer the most basic questions.

It was Lyle the police were relying on to tell the story of what had happened to their parents. What seemed peculiar to the detectives was how different the two brothers were. Lyle was able to relate what happened and was under complete control in answering questions. Granted, he was 2½ years older than Erik, but he was totally composed and answered every question. When asked what they had done during the day, Lyle started out telling them about playing tennis with his brother. There was mention that Erik had several days before returned from a series of tennis tournaments and was preparing to attend UCLA.

Lyle went on to explain that they had gone shopping at the Beverly Center because he wanted to get some things before leaving the next day for Princeton. After the shopping trip, they drove out to Santa Monica for the 'Taste of L.A.,' a local food festival. By 8:00 p.m., several of them decided to go to the movies in Westwood Village next to UCLA. Most students who have attended UCLA can attest to how often the ticket line extended around the block. So the brothers decided to go over to the Century City Mall Theatre, where they readily got in to see ***Batman***.

When the movie was over, their group of friends wanted to get something to eat. They all agreed to meet at the Cheesecake Factory in Beverly Hills. Lyle was then slightly reluctant to tell the detective that they decided to come home to pick up Erik's fake ID so he could buy beer at the restaurant. He knew the police might confiscate the fake ID, but he was trying to be as candid as he could possibly be.

But what Lyle said next caused the police to think twice. Lyle explained they had walked into the house and they detected a strong smoky smell. It seemed strongest when they entered the family room. That was when they noticed their parents had been shot. The detectives were taking notes and seemed perplexed by the statement of the smell of smoke. In the detective's experience, the smoke that occurs when shooting a shotgun generally dissipates quickly so it seemed highly unlikely this would be detected when they claimed they entered the family room without seeing the shooters.

When they were asked as to who might want to commit such an act they claimed they had no idea. Lyle did relate to the detective that their mother was extremely depressed and had attempted suicide by overdosing on drugs. The detectives didn't know what to make of his claim that their mother was suicidal. Based on viewing the crime scene there was no evidence that made this shooting look like a suicide.

After several hours of questioning, the final question was whether the brothers had any idea who would have shot their parents. Lyle shook his head indicating he had no idea, then stated, "Maybe the mob did it." This caught the detectives totally off guard, as they wondered why a son would suspect the mob of killing their parents. The detective remembered that both bodies did have their kneecaps shot off. That was a common trademark of a 'mob hit.'

The detective terminated the interview and told the brothers they were free to leave but they may need to talk to them more in the future, if more questions arose. The police didn't consider them suspects at that time, so they didn't even ask to have their hands checked for Gun Shot Residue (GSR). This is a test that can show if a person recently fired a gun. Most likely, the brothers had thoroughly washed their hands before calling the police. However this type of forensic test might have been highly revealing, unfortunately we will never know the results of such a test since it was never conducted.

On the following graphic page are photos of the Menendez house on the night of the shooting.

Graphic 10

MENENDEZ BEVERLY HILLS HOME

Lyle's red car in car court

Front Door

Foyer

Stairs in Foyer

Living room

CHAPTER 36 MONTHS AFTER SHOOTING

Since their parents' house had been turned into a crime scene, the brothers decided to move into the Beverly Hills Hotel, several blocks away. (Over the years, this historic hotel had been the temporary home for many visiting movie stars.)

It was unclear which brother had come up with the idea that whoever had killed their parents was possibly after them too. They made it seem that it was either a mob hit or some other business group that was out to kill them as well. Lyle hired bodyguards to follow him around when they went out. By September, Lyle told the bodyguards that he no longer needed their services since his uncle had made peace with the mob. It was never explained to anyone how his uncle had worked out an arrangement with organized crime, but that was the end of the bodyguards.

Shortly after the victims' bodies were released from the Coroner's Office, the family had an elaborate memorial service at the Directors Guild of America in Los Angeles. Both brothers attended the service. Lyle was completely composed, while Erik seemed emotionally upset and appeared very withdrawn. Then on August 28, 1989, the entire set of Menendez and Anderson relatives gathered at the Princeton University Chapel for another memorial service. What was most memorable about this event was the fact that Lyle rose to the occasion and gave one of the most glowing eulogies about his beloved parents. He spoke for over 30 minutes, praising their virtues and what magnificent parents they had been. He told the crowd how much his father had taught him while growing up. He explained how much he admired his dad for all he had accomplished and what he had given his sons. He expressed a special fondness for their mother, who had done so much in raising them to be the fine young men they had become.

There wasn't a dry eye at the service, and no son could have heaped more praise on his parents for all their love and sacrifice they had given. Afterwards, the bodies were buried at the local Princeton Cemetery, where eventually a large headstone was erected over their graves. Lyle wanted to prove to everyone that he was taking control of the family interests. Instead of returning to Princeton to finish his education, he decided to return to Los Angeles to straighten things out for the family. Erik, who took a backseat in everything, had decided not to attend UCLA and returned to Los Angeles to get on with his life.

After running up a hefty bill at the Beverly Hills Hotel, the brothers rented two separate apartments in Marina Del Rey, each one costing $5,800 a month. Apparently, the brothers had been watching too many ***Baywatch*** episodes with Pamela Anderson running, or more correctly, bouncing across the sandy beach. That TV program was top on the charts in 1989. The brothers wanted to have the most magnificent place at the beach so they could have a place to entertain the 'beach bunnies.' They put a down payment on a luxurious suite on the top floor of the complex, but since neither brother had a job, the purchase was rejected.

At first Lyle used his father's American Express card and charged $90,000 for purchases. The brothers needed access to more money, and somehow they were able to obtain funds from their dad's life insurance for a total of $650,000. That was the cash cow that allowed them to go on a wild spending spree. They spent $15,000 on Rolex watches, which they needed in order to be on time wherever they had to be. They purchased thousands of dollars' worth of designer clothes so they could look their best if they happen to go on a job interview.

The one thing Lyle wanted the most was a new car. He was always resentful of having to drive the red Alfa Romeo convertible sports car that he was given for his high school graduation. He went to the Beverly Hills Porsche dealership, where he could find a genuine sportsman's vehicle. He selected a Carrera 911 costing $64,000. Lyle looked the part of a mover and shaker in the business world. He eventually returned to the Princeton area, where he created Menendez Investment Enterprises. He encouraged a number of his college friends to join him in this business. No one had any business experience, and the venture turned into a money pit, throwing good money after bad money.

Lyle had always wanted to operate a restaurant. So he looked around the Princeton community to see what type of establishment would be successful. He decided to purchase Chuck's Spring Street Café for $550,000 and immediately changed the name to 'Mr. Buffalo.' The business struggled. It was never known why the business was failing; maybe it was because his friends were eating up the profits. The bottom line was the restaurant did nothing except lose money. It was important for Lyle to project an image of success, so he continued to tell people the restaurant was going to expand all over the USA, near all major college campuses.

Lyle was busy commuting back and forth between the coasts. Erik, on the other hand, recognized he wasn't going to excel at business or as a student. He decided to pursue other goals and hired a tennis coach to accompany him to various tournaments around the world. He spent over $60,000 on the services of a tennis coach. It was amazing how the two brothers were able to spend over a million dollars within a six-month period since their parents' deaths.

The brothers hired attorneys and accountants to determine the extent of their parents' estate. By adding up all the family assets, the total came to about $14,000,000, and after subtracting the indebtedness, it would leave the brothers both about $2 million. The brothers were extremely disappointed since they had expected much more. They had an expectation they would be sharing $90,000,000. The brothers were certain their father, Jose, had put money in a Swiss bank account. The question was, which Swiss bank was it?

What's ironic was that in the Billionaire Boys Club case, Joe Hunt was disappointed with the amount of money in Ron Levin's Swiss account. Then there was Hedayat, who was thought to have $30 million in Swiss bank accounts, which turned out to be only several thousand dollars. It seemed that Swiss bank accounts had disappointed a number of ***Rich Kid Killers of Beverly Hills***.

CHAPTER 37 INVESTIGATION

There are very few homicides that occur in Beverly Hills, but when they do happen, they can be the most difficult to solve. Det. Zoeller had eliminated the usual causes of homicides such as a burglary or robbery that had gone bad. Initially he was surprised at how many of Jose's friends and business colleagues had stories to tell about how driven he was. Jose didn't get to the top by tiptoeing around. Some of his business dealings could be described by some as ruthless. The investigators interviewed all the neighbors and associates in Beverly Hills, and then turned their attention to the people in Calabasas, who had known the Menendez family as neighbors when they were living in the Valley.

Det. Zoeller contacted a Peter and Karen Wright, who said something unexpected that shocked the police. Peter said, "I have no basis for this, but I wonder if the boys did it." Zoeller asked, "Why would you suspect the brothers?" They then related the brothers all of sudden seemed overly polite and pleasant, far from how they had acted when their parents were alive. Zoeller pondered this information. He knew this wasn't evidence but could there be a link between the brothers and the killings? What gave this little speculation some legs was the fact that the brothers had been on a spending spree, and it wasn't going unnoticed by people in Beverly Hills. However, Zoeller had seen so many children go through their inheritance in a short time, especially Rich Kids in Beverly Hills. He chalked this up to a natural tendency that Rich Kids often revert to 'Spendthrifts.'

The detectives were contacted by one of Lyle's best friends, Glen Stone (pseudonym), who added an odd twist to the investigation. He indicated that Lyle had told him a strange story about how he and his brother had hired a computer expert to look into Kitty's computer. In particular, they were interested in any files regarding his parents changing their wills. Lyle said to Stone, days after the shootings, that they had taken their mother's computer to a computer expert to eliminate any files regarding a change to their parents' wills. It was a successful venture for the brothers and now no one would be able to find any new will disinheriting them.

Glen said Lyle was trying to manipulate Erik so Lyle would get all, or at least most of the money from the estate. It sounded like GREED was setting in between the brothers. Det. Zoeller knew from experience that GREED often was the wedge that could crack open a case and make people more willing to talk. Therefore, Det. Zoeller called Erik and told him there were some loose ends he wanted to discuss with him.

On October 24, 1989, Zoeller and his partner met Erik at the family mansion, where he was staying with his grandmother. They met in the living room and had a pleasant enough meeting. Since Lyle was back in Princeton working on his new restaurant business, Erik had no one to support or advise him. The detectives reviewed some of the information they had received during the investigation. Zoeller said he was sorry Erik wasn't getting along with his brother. This may have caught

Erik off guard. He replied that he didn't like the manner in which Lyle was spending all the money. He even went on to say he didn't like the way Lyle was treating him. He said, "He treats me just like my dad did." After an hour of questions, the detectives thanked Erik for meeting with them and then they left.

Erik was the younger brother, who was overly sensitive and also lacked self-confidence in dealing with others. After the meeting, Erik started thinking of what he had told the detectives and wondered if he had said too much. He needed to talk to someone who could give him reassurance that he hadn't done anything wrong. He knew Lyle was consumed with his new restaurant business. So who could he turn to? Since he and his brother had killed their parents, he couldn't ask for advice from his mom or dad. Then he remembered the psychiatrist who he had worked with as part of the sentence for the Calabasas burglaries.

CHAPTER 38 MEETING WITH PSYCHIATRIST

Erik fortunately was able to get an appointment with Dr. Jerome Owens. On October 31, 1989, he met with his psychiatrist at his office in Beverly Hills. The doctor could see how depressed Erik was, even showing signs of suicidal ideation. To calm him down, Dr. Owens suggested walking around the block might help him. Since it was Halloween and some of the people of Beverly Hills were running around in various costumes, he thought it might be a distraction for Erik.

Some office workers were suited up in scary pirate outfits. Since it was the year for Ninja Warriors, several kids dressed up as Teenage Mutant Ninja Turtles as passersbys smile approvingly. As they approached a building on Wilshire Blvd., it looked like two secretaries had decided to come to work as Elvira. Maybe they were planning to scare their bosses with their slinky dresses and push-up bras. Everything was upbeat until Erik and his psychiatrist came around a corner and saw a theater marquee announcing one of the Halloween Chainsaw Massacre movies.

The psychiatrist had to have second thoughts as to the wisdom of walking around the block in Beverly Hills on Halloween. Just by looking at Erik's face, the psychiatrist knew something was truly wrong. Erik appeared detached, as though he had something on his mind. The psychiatrist kept asking probing questions, trying to open up the conversation so Erik would reveal what was bothering him. All of a sudden, Erik stopped on the sidewalk and wrapped his arm around a parking meter for some type of support. He looked directly at Dr. Owens and said in a timid, fearful voice, "**We did it. We killed our parents.**"

It was unclear who had the most surprised look on their face. Dr. Owens had learned through psychiatry school that a professional must not show any emotion, no matter what the patient says. He was trying to keep his composure and merely suggested this was a good time to return to his office. As they headed back, Erik was like a volcano that had erupted. He started spewing out justifications for the killings. He explained it was the fault, or result of, **watching the Billionaire Boys Club TV mini-series,** which gave them the idea to kill their folks. It seemed like the killing was not their fault, but that the TV mini-series should somehow be blamed since it planted the seed that resulted in their parents' deaths.

Erik said that after watching the mini-series, he and his brother talked about their belief that their parents were disinheriting them. They complained about how their dad dominated their lives. They rationalized the killing of their father, then realized their mother would have to be killed since she couldn't live without her husband. Dr. Owens had a sinking feeling that he was in over his head. Thinking back to med school, he tried to remember what to do when a patient admits to a crime.

He didn't know where this was going. His first thought was that he needed some form of verification of what Erik was saying. Then he asked Erik if his brother, Lyle, was available. Erik indicated he didn't know but he would try to call him. Fortunately, Erik was able to reach Lyle, who had returned from the East Coast. Dr.

Owens told Erik to invite his brother over to the psychiatrist's Beverly Hills office, to which Lyle agreed.

Erik was like a broken dam with the water roaring out. He couldn't stop talking about the killings. He volunteered that they wanted to commit the perfect crime. They decided to go all the way to San Diego to purchase the shotguns from a Big 5 Sporting Goods store. Erik related how he had used the identification from his brother's old friend, Donovan Guthman. By using Donovan's identification, the shotguns couldn't be traced back to the brothers.

Almost as if he were bragging, he showed how smart they had been since they picked up all the expended shotgun shells and removed them so they wouldn't have their fingerprints on them. For Erik, it was therapeutic for him to reveal to the psychiatrist all the sophisticated thinking the two of them had exhibited. He said that after the shooting they noticed a slight amount of blood spatter on their clothes and shoes. As a result, they went upstairs to their and changed their clothes.

Almost in a bragging tone, Erik went on to explain how ingenious they were that on the following evening they disposed of the shotguns by driving up to Mulholland Drive. On one of the dark secluded curves, they pulled over onto the shoulder and stopped Lyle's Alfa Romeo. They both stepped out and proceeded to the trunk. Without feeling any attachment to the shotguns, they each grabbed one and briskly walked over to the edge of the cliff. One by one, the brothers threw the shotguns far down into the steep brushy slope. In the silence of the night, they could hear the slight clanging of the shotguns striking the boulders as they tumbled into oblivion. (For years, law enforcement has searched all along Mulholland Drive and have never found any trace of the shotguns.)

It wasn't clear whether Erik was trying to impress his psychiatrist or just trying to gain his approval. He went on to explain how the two of them drove down into the city area and looked for a service station. Eventually they found one and Lyle pulled into the rear area where a trash dumpster was pushed up against a block wall. Again they went to the trunk and carefully picked up all the expended shell casings and walked over to the trash dumpster and tossed them in. Returning to the trunk, they picked up their bloody clothes and shoes and likewise threw them away like trash.

Erik seemed to feel a certain degree of relief in sharing this burden that he had been holding within himself. Within the hour, Lyle arrived at Dr. Owens's office. When he found out that Erik had told the psychiatrist everything, he became furious. He didn't know how to react since part of committing 'the perfect crime' also included not telling anyone. Lyle seemed to settle down and then made the following statement: "My dad would have been proud of me in committing such an effective murder."

Dr. Owens didn't know what his role should be, with all this boasting as to how smart they were in pulling off these murders. He thought his role was to explain to them the various states of mind involved in a homicide case. So, he tried to explain the difference between murder and manslaughter. He explained that a person who planned it would be a sociopath versus a spur-of-the-moment type killing. The brothers looked at each other and declared they must be sociopathic. The session was coming to an end. Erik was feeling better and relieved, while Lyle was still irate at Erik for letting the cat out of the bag.

As Lyle was about to leave, he turned to Dr. Owens and said, in no uncertain terms, "You had better not tell anybody what we just told." The good doctor assured them that his lips were sealed because of the psychiatrist-patient relationship. Lyle made it very clear that he would kill him if he said anything to anyone.

On November 2, 1989, the brothers had another meeting with Dr. Owens. When Lyle arrived, he said to Dr. Owens they had been considering whether or not to kill him since they wanted to keep the killings a secret. Dr. Owens was able to reassure them that their secret was safe with him. The brothers continued to 'tell all' about what happened as Dr. Owens tried to help them deal with all their fears and depression. The brothers must have thought this therapy was helpful for them, so they continued to have more therapeutic sessions with the psychiatrist over the next several weeks.

CHAPTER 39 THE WRATH OF A WOMAN SCORNED

The detectives hadn't uncovered any hard evidence. As the fall of 1989 turned to the winter of 1990, some wondered if the Menendez murders would ever be solved. There wasn't anything more than mere suspicion as the brothers continued to spend money as quickly as it was printed. Was anyone happy? The **Beverly Hills Police Department wasn't showing any signs of happiness**. They were feeling the pressure from the community because they weren't clever enough to solve the one homicide case they had in 1989. Apparently, **Lyle was happy** since he was a big businessman in Princeton with his Mr. Buffalo Restaurant. **Erik was happy** since he had a tennis coach who had helped him improve his game and was traveling the world, participating in various tournaments.

Dr. Owens seemed happy in that nothing bad had happened to him. As a matter of fact, he was happy to have an attractive girlfriend, Jordan Shay (pseudonym), who was 37 years old and had gorgeous red hair. She had previously been a patient of Dr. Owens and had evolved from patient to mistress. Dr. Owens never felt comfortable around the brothers since they had told him they had thought about killing him. The good doctor believed he couldn't reveal to anyone what the brothers had admitted to doing. He didn't want to irritate them to the point where they would come after him. However, they continued to have sessions with him in which he felt obligated to comply with them to ensure his own safety.

Then Dr. Owens came up with the idea that, for his safety, he would have his girlfriend hide in the back office so she could hear any threats of things they might try to do to him. Whenever there was a therapy session with the brothers, she would eavesdrop from the back room. The area she was located in was the perfect spot. She could hear the brothers talking between themselves and with Dr. Owens. At one point, Erik said to his brother, "I can't stop you from what you have to do, but I can't kill any more." Erick ran out of that session, but Lyle remained and said to the psychiatrist, "I can kind of understand Erik, but he shouldn't have done this." Later, Dr. Owens told the brothers that he would help them to better understand the 'family' history and how it may have contributed to them killing their parents.

The months passed by and the brothers continued to live the good life as a Rich Kid in Beverly Hills. Dr. Owens enjoyed the constant companionship of his girlfriend. But as time went by, Dr. Owens apparently lost interest in his red-headed girlfriend, who had acted as his security every time he had a session with the brothers. The good doctor may have found a younger damsel, so he told Jordan her services were no longer needed. Possibly, the psychiatrist had forgotten several ethical rules of his profession, which included no fraternizing with patients. Also, he was not allowed to have others listen in on therapy sessions.

There is an old saying that applies here, which is ***"Hell hath no fury like a woman scorned."*** (This expression is derived from Willian Congreve, a playwright way back in 1700, and certainly still applies today). The girlfriend looked at the hand the good doctor had dealt her. When Dr. Owens didn't return her phone calls and completely avoided her, she thought his behavior was so unfair, considering all she had gone through trying to protect him. Then one day she felt she had been offended enough and decided to take action that would hurt Dr. Owens. She had no malice toward the Menendez brothers; they would merely be 'Collateral Damage.'

She picked up the phone and dialed the Beverly Hills Police Department, asking to speak to the detectives investigating the Menendez killings. She told them she had overheard the Menendez brothers explain *how* they killed their parents. The detectives couldn't believe their ears. They had put in thousands of investigative hours and still had nothing to date to justify arresting the brothers. Here, the mistress (possibility ex-mistress) of a psychiatrist, held all the aces in this case.

She explained there were audio tapes and notes that spelled everything out. The detectives had to believe that Christmas had come early for them that year. They asked her if she would come in so they could have a little chat. Within a short time, she was explaining exactly how the brothers had described the killings. She said the brothers bought shotguns in San Diego and threw them over into the thick brush along Mulholland Drive. She told them there were tapes of the conversations and lengthy notes.

At that point, the excitement in the room of detectives was greater than finding out that they had the winning numbers for the MegaMillions Lottery. What could be better than tapes of the brothers admitting to their crimes? The ecstatic feeling of the detectives was soon shattered as they were advised the tapes might be considered to be *privileged* under the psychotherapist- patient law. The euphoria was over, and Detective Zoeller said it was time to contact the district attorney's office for some legal advice.

Elliot Alhatfoff and Pamela Bozanich from the L.A. County DA's Office were contacted and brought in for guidance. It was decided they would obtain a search warrant to find out for certain what they had. First, they located a judge, who signed the search warrant and assigned a Special Master (this is a person appointed by a judge to make sure that judicial orders are strictly followed) to assist in the search. Since these tapes involved a psychotherapist and patient, the court required any tapes located to be given to the Special Master to bring into court for a judge to decide if the *privilege* applied.

The detectives and Special Master went to Dr. Owens's home. They had to wait a few minutes before he arrived with his attorney. The detectives advised Dr. Owens that they were there to seize audio tapes regarding the Menendez brothers. The detectives explained there were two ways of doing the search: either the doctor could turn over all his tapes and notes, or they could turn his house and office upside down looking for the items. The good doctor may have realized this time he was way in over his head. He took the approach of trying to appear helpful in hopes that maybe the authorities would go easy on him.

The doctor huddled with his attorney for a few minutes, then came back to the detectives and told them the tapes were in a safe deposit box in a bank. The tricky thing was, the detectives didn't know the name or location of the bank he was referring to, therefore, they had not requested to search any such site. The detectives made it clear they had a valid search warrant for the tapes and the doctor could see they were clearly listed on the search warrant. Dr. Owens said he could take the detectives to the bank where the tapes were stored. Everyone agreed, and Dr. Owens told them it was a bank in the San Fernando Valley.

The all got into their vehicles and traveled to the bank. The bank manager had to be surprised when this crowd of detectives, attorneys, a Special Master, and psychiatrist arrived and asked to go into the vault and retrieve a safe deposit box. The bank staff had to wonder why all these people were viewing this one safe deposit box. In order to be satisfied that these were the tapes involving the Menendez brothers, the detective asked for them to be played, with everyone present in the bank's safety deposit room.

Dr. Owens felt he had the upper hand now since he knew which tapes contained the brothers' voices admitting to the killing of their parents. He had a tape player and put in one of the tapes. The "Play" button was pushed and after some preliminary talking there came the voice of Lyle Menendez, admitting how they bought the shotguns in San Diego. Lyle went on to explain that they had to go back to his car to reload the shotguns with birdshot to finish off their mother. In this little bank safe deposit room, if there had been a 'fly on the wall' it would have fainted after hearing this bombshell confession by the brothers.

The detectives wanted to high five each other but tried to show restraint by placing every tape into an evidence envelope, with a description on it, then sealing and turning it over to the Special Master, who took custody of the 17 audio tapes. The DA's Office said they would ask the judge to instruct the Special Master to have all the tapes transcribed so their admissibility could be litigated in court.

Later on, Detective Zoeller received information from Craig Curry, a friend of the brothers. Craig told the police he had a conversation with Erik in which he had told him how the killing actually went down. Erik told Craig he and his brother had returned to the house so Erik could obtain his fake ID. When he returned to the car, Lyle had the shotguns out and said, "Let's do it." They both went to the back of the house and entered. (Even though the brothers didn't have a key to the house, they had learned how to sneak in through one of the den doors that couldn't be securely locked.) They quietly slipped into the family room. They found their folks had fallen asleep on the sofa. Lyle went behind his dad and shot him. Erik said he was supposed to shoot his mother, but he couldn't do it, so Lyle shot her. Later, Erik said he then shot his mother twice in the face.

Det. Zoeller recognized that Craig's story of Erik explanation was different from what the brothers said on the tapes. Craig said he didn't know whether to believe Erik or not. He said many times Erik would play these "word games." The detectives contacted the DA's Office and asked to see if Craig would wear a wire. To everyone's surprise, Craig agreed. The police wired Craig for sound when he went to meet Erik for dinner at Gladstone's 4 Fish on Pacific Coast Highway. This is an eating establishment where the legendary Sunset Blvd. ends at the Pacific Ocean. The view from the patio of the ocean is breathtaking, as are the sandy beaches where movie stars and celebrities hang out. This seemed like a good meeting place, far enough from Beverly Hills that it wouldn't attract any attention.

Craig was seated in a quiet corner of the restaurant when Erik came in and sat across from him at the table. They spent considerable time with small talk as they had a drink. When Craig thought it was time to ask about how his parents were killed, he asked about the version Erik had told him about his involvement. Erik's response was he had nothing to do with his parents' murders. When Craig tried to refresh Erik's memory of what he had told him, Erik said that if he had said it, he was lying. Erik didn't want to talk about his parents' deaths. Everyone was disappointed when Erik didn't take the bait, but it was at least worth a try.

CHAPTER 40 TIME FOR ARRESTS

Lyle was in Princeton working at his Mr. Buffalo restaurant when he decided to fly back to L.A. He had learned Det. Zoeller was looking for him. After he landed in L.A., he went to the family mansion on Elm Street where his father's mother, Maria Menendez, was staying. On March 8, Lyle was leaving the house and driving Erik's jeep. He pulled out heading southbound on Elm when he saw a car with a flashing light. As he got closer, it looked to him like an undercover police car and he immediately jammed on the brakes. In one motion he put the jeep in reverse, with tires squealing, and started backing up until there was a loud clunk. He looked in the rear view mirror and saw a large police van behind him.

By that time, there were police officers completely surrounding the jeep. Lyle had nowhere to go except to get out with his hands up, and was immediately handcuffed. The next thing he remembered was being in a lockup cell at the Sheriff's West Hollywood Station. Later in the day, he was transported to the Men's County Jail. By that afternoon, District Attorney Ira Reiner was holding a news conference announcing the arrest of Lyle Menendez for the murder of his parents. When asked what the reason was for the murders, the DA said, "I don't know what your experience is, but it's been our experience in the district attorney's office that $14 million provides ample motive for someone to kill somebody." DA Reiner also indicated that Special Circumstances had been added to the charges, making Lyle eligible for the Death Penalty.

The police had one of the brothers, but the other one was free as a bird out of the country. Erik was participating in a tennis tournament that was taking place in Israel. He was faced with the most monumental decision of his life. He had his American passport and could have easily left Israel and traveled to a dozen other countries that didn't have extradition treaties with the USA. An example was the Philippines, where he could have gone and been safe from extradition. With the money he had access to, Erik could have lived well for the rest of his life wherever he decided to go, as long as he traveled wisely through the proper country.

Erik called his uncle, who advised him to come home and get the matter cleared up. His relatives couldn't image either brother being involved in their parents' deaths. They honestly believed it was a mere misunderstanding that would be worked out in a very short time. So Erik followed his uncle's advice and took a plane to Miami, where he met his aunt who would fly with him to LAX. When he landed, Detective Zoeller was there to greet him and arrest him, thereby taking him into custody.

Now the easy part was over and the police were congratulating themselves. The DA's office now had to figure out what ADMISSIBLE evidence they had to prosecute both brothers.

CHAPTER 41 BUILDING A CASE

The DA's Office decided to charge the two brothers with two counts of murder. One count for each parent, with three special circumstance allegations for 'Multiple Murder,' 'Lying In Wait,' and 'For Financial Gain.' There was a third charge of Conspiracy to commit Murder, which was added on for tactical reasons. The crimes had occurred several blocks from the Beverly Hills courthouse, so it made it the proper location for an arraignment of the case. Since both brothers were in custody at the same place, they were transported to the Beverly Hills courthouse from the county jail in Sheriff's vans.

Judge Stein was assigned to conduct the arraignment. The brothers had been in custody for about two weeks, and this was their first opportunity to be seen by the public and family members. They were ushered into the courtroom by Sheriff's deputies and seated at the counsel table. They turned their heads so they could look at the audience, then fixated on certain friends and family members and waved to them like they were some type of rock stars. Both brothers had big smiles, as though it was an old class reunion and they were proud to show others how well they had done.

The Menendez and Anderson (their mother's) families were there in force to support them. The families viewed the whole thing as being an unfortunate mistake that would be ironed out in a matter of days. The families had hired the best attorneys their daddy's money could buy. The judge took the bench and asked the brothers to stand so she could read the charges to them. Erik looked at this older, petite, female judge, who had a peculiar way of letting her glasses slide down her nose. To Erik, this was a peculiar sight and he started giggling, almost uncontrollably. Lyle started breaking up and couldn't stop laughing, so he started covering his mouth with his hand.

Judge Stein didn't seem to notice, since her attention was directed at the packed courtroom with all the media. In a monotone voice, she started reading the charges and, when she was finished she turned to the defendants and said, "How do you plea?" At that point, each of their attorneys whispered in their ear for them to say "Not Guilty," which each of them obediently recited. Next, each of their attorneys was asked by the judge what date they wanted for the preliminary hearing. There was consulting back and forth and finally a date was agreed to.

So began one of the longest cases in the Los Angeles County criminal justice system. Erik was represented by Leslie Abramson, who without a doubt was the most cantankerous and abrasive attorney the courts have ever known. Her shortness and her little Orphan Annie hairdo made her easily identifiable. She had been a public defender who had gained considerable experience on a number of publicity cases. She detested the Death Penalty, and since this was set up as a possible Death Penalty case, this was the type of case she personally and fervently liked to handle. Also, the $750,000 she was paid from Jose's estate was appreciated, even though Jose would not have cherished how she turned him into a villain and the person responsible for their own murders.

Lyle was represented by Jill Lansing, another former public defender attorney who had become a private attorney. She was well respected and wasn't used to doing publicity cases, although she was very capable.

From the prosecution side, Pam Ferrero Bozanich was named as the lead attorney for the DA's Office. Her career had included finishing up the McMartin case, which had been an albatross around the DA Office's neck. She had worked with David Conn on the Bill Bradford serial killer case, in which the DA's Offices sought the Death Penalty. Pam Bozanich would primarily be responsible for presenting the evidence against Lyle, while her co-counsel, Lester Kuriyama, was primarily responsible for Erik's jury trial. Lester had been involved in some lengthy cases and was well seasoned.

The case was set in Beverly Hills for the preliminary hearing; however, there was a legal battle brewing that could delay the case for years as it percolated all the way to the California Supreme Court. The DA's Office was relying on having all the tapes and notes from Dr. Owens held admissible so the jury could hear them. A hearing on the admissibility was held in the Santa Monica court by Judge James Albrecht. The Defense strenuously objected to all of Dr. Owens's material since it was obtained in violation of the **California Evidence Code Section 1014, which provides "The patient, whether or not a party, has a privilege to refuse to disclose and to prevent another from disclosing, *a confidential communication between patient and psychotherapist..."*** Both brothers claimed they were patients of Dr. Owens, a psychotherapist, and anything they told him was considered a confidential communication.

Several of the tapes involved Dr. Owens's dictation of notes regarding the therapy sessions with the brothers. One tape of the brothers described how and why they killed their parents. The judge agreed the statements and information were definitely Privileged Communications and came within the restraints of Section 1014.

But the prosecution argued there was an exception that applied and allowed the statements to be admissible under certain circumstance as described in **California Evidence Code Section 1024, which provides "There is *no privilege* under this article if the psychotherapist has reasonable cause to believe that the *patient is in such mental or emotional conditions* as to be *Dangerous* to himself or *the person* or property of others and that disclosure of communication is necessary to prevent the threatened danger."**

On August 6, 1990, Judge James Albrecht ruled that the threats Lyle made to Dr. Owens erased the patient-therapist confidentiality barrier and it was necessary to disclose those communications to prevent the threatened danger and ordered the tapes be given to the DA. Erik's attorney, Leslie Abramson, took the matter up to the appellate court, and that court overturned Judge Albrecht's decision and ruled that no tapes could be released or used in court. The Defense was elated and there was no way the DA could obtain a conviction against either brother without those tapes.

Generally, the DA's Office doesn't take an appeal all the way to the California Supreme Court. However, this case had generated hard feelings because some thought these Rich Kids were going to get away with murder just because they had the money to hire expensive attorneys to get them off. Therefore, the DA's Office had no choice but to continue the fight all the way to the top court. On August 27, 1992, the Supreme Court made a compromise ruling.

"The court held that the dangerous patient exception applied to the first tape, since the therapist had reasonable cause to believe that the brothers were dangerous to himself directly and to his wife and lover collaterally, and that disclosure to the two women was necessary to prevent any harm." As to the second and third tapes, the court held that the communications were made within the course of therapy, and thus the privilege applied. It also held that the dangerous patient exception did not apply to these two tapes since the therapist had no reasonable cause to believe that the disclosure of any communication made during these sessions was necessary to prevent harm.

The bottom line was that the DA's Office was still in the race to prosecute both, but they wouldn't be able to use the best tape, which had the defendants' voices on it describing how they did the killings. Dr. Owens could testify as to the first session when Lyle made the threat to kill him if he said anything to the police.

All this legal wrangling consumed three years, while the brothers languished in county jail. What was most interesting was how the Defense in the case pivoted on this Supreme Court decision. The days before the Supreme Court ruling, the Defense's position was:

WE DIDN'T KILL OUR PARENTS

Believe us – we are being unjustly accused of a crime we didn't commit

The day after the Supreme Court ruling, the Defense's position had changed 180 degrees:

YES, WE KILLED OUR PARENTS

But we had to do it since they were going to kill us

Believe us - we are the victims in this case

People from outside the US often wonder why Americans like to claim **trials are a search for the truth.** It may seem peculiar to them how the question as to what is the ***truth*** isn't an absolute but is relative to how one wants to spin the facts.

After the decision that the one tape would come in, the DA's Office tried to have a preliminary hearing, which continued to be delayed. The case had been delayed for years, and the DA's Office wasn't going to accept more delays. The possibility of all the witnesses being lost or the witnesses' memories fading over time was becoming a real concern. Subsequently, the DA's Office took the case to the Grand Jury in downtown L.A. and got an indictment against both defendants for two counts of murder with special circumstances of Multiple Murder and Lying In Wait. However, the grand jurors didn't approve the special circumstances of 'Murder for Financial Gain.' That seemed odd since the motive had been to prevent the parents from cutting the brothers out of their parents' wills. The DA didn't argue with the Grand Jury as to why they had rejected the Financial Gains allegation. They also tacked on a charge of Conspiracy to Commit Murder.

The case was assigned to Judge Stanley Weisberg, a downtown judge who was about to be transferred to the Van Nuys courthouse. He was a methodical and scholarly judge. He was bald and had wire rim glasses that made him look nerdy. He had received considerable attention when he was the judge in the Rodney King case, in the Simi Valley in 1992. That case involved four white police officers who had attacked Mr. King, a black man, during an arrest. In that case, all the officers were acquitted, and the result was the most violent riot in L.A.'s history. Many people were killed and injured, many businesses were destroyed, and much of the midsection of L.A. was burned down.

CHAPTER 42 FIRST TRIAL

By May of 1993, the groundwork had been laid for the Menendez Brothers trial to begin in Judge Weisberg's courtroom in Van Nuys Superior Court. The legal issue was whether the two brothers should be tried together or separately. Since the prosecution wanted to use the statements by both brothers, there would be a need to have separate juries to decide the case against each brother. The prosecution can't use a statement by one defendant that incriminates another defendant. However, after the judge reviewed the list of witnesses, he realized they were basically all the same.

The judge, who wanted to save court time, came up with the idea of having **two separate juries sitting in on one trial**. When the statement of one defendant would be introduced, the other defendant's jury would be excused and not hear that testimony. Although this sounds like a good idea, in that you don't have to have two separate trials, it also creates all sorts of logistic problems. The obvious question, was where do you seat the second jury of 12 jurors and six alternates? It was worked out by using a portion of the spectators' seats. Everyone would agree the courtroom was cozy. Since there were two separate juries, there had to be two separate sets of exhibits, complicating the work of the courtroom clerk.

When they started selecting the juries, there were 1,100 potential jurors summoned to the courthouse for consideration. They were given a questionnaire containing 122 questions they had to fill out and turn in. One of the areas the attorneys on both sides wanted to know about was what TV programs the jurors watched. This was the time in history when the top TV programs were ***Seinfeld*, *ER*, *Home Improvement*, and *Friends,*** but that didn't say anything about the potential juror. However, the programs ***60 Minutes, NYPD Blue, Murder She Wrote, and Law and Order*** did say something about the type of juror they were considering. Since the *Hovey* opinion, all the jurors had to be interviewed separately. It was a lengthy process and it wasn't until July 20, 1993, that in Lyle's case they had selected a jury of seven men and five women, and in Erik's case they had a jury of eight men and four women.

Since the two juries occupied so much space in the courtroom, the press complained there weren't enough seats for all the journalists, many of whom had traveled from all over the world. Judge Weisberg recognized the limited space issue and agreed that a TV camera could be placed in the courtroom that would permit the extra journalists to be able to cover the trial from another room. This was the origin for TV's gavel-to-gavel coverage. The Joe Hunt case involved a TV camera in the courtroom, but it didn't provide for a live broadcast, as was planned in the Menendez case.

Shortly before the start of the trial, Erik's attorney, Leslie Abramson, gave an interview in which she laid out the Defense's strategy of the brothers' cases. She explained how they were going to call experts who would tell the jury it was the parents who sexually and mentally abused their sons to a point where the brothers believed their parents were about to kill them, so, in self-defense, the brothers shot and killed their parents first.

The brothers' Defense was based on Paul Mones' book, "When a Child Kills: Abused Children Who Kill Their Parents." In those situations, a child struck back by overkilling. They claimed that was what happened in this case. Both Defense attorneys had the brothers dress in juvenile clothing such as sweaters, sport shirts, and khaki pants. They wanted to project the image the brothers were merely confused teenagers.

The brothers had the unwavering support of their grandmother, Maria Menendez, and their aunts, Marta Cano and Terry Brewer. However, no one from the Anderson (Kitty's) side of the family continued to support the boys with their new story of abusive parents.

The following graphic page shows the evidence and people involved in the first trial.

FIRST MENENDEZ TRIAL

Psychiatrist had 17 tapes

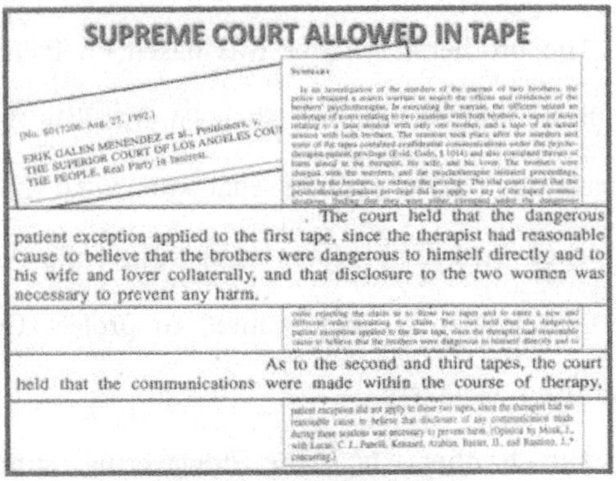
SUPREME COURT ALLOWED IN TAPE

(No. S017206. Aug. 27, 1992.)

ERIK GALEN MENENDEZ et al., Petitioners, v.
THE SUPERIOR COURT OF LOS ANGELES COU
THE PEOPLE, Real Party in Interest.

. The court held that the dangerous patient exception applied to the first tape, since the therapist had reasonable cause to believe that the brothers were dangerous to himself directly and to his wife and lover collaterally, and that disclosure to the two women was necessary to prevent any harm.

As to the second and third tapes, the court held that the communications were made within the course of therapy,

One tape could be used in trial

548

FILED

Grand Jury Indictment

Trial Judge Stanley Weisberg

Pamela Bozanich | Detective Les Zoeller | Lester Kuriyama

Brothers crying on the witness stand

Graphic 11

CHAPTER 43 FIRST TRIAL—OPENING STATEMENTS

On July 20, 1993, Prosecutor Pam Bozanich was asked by the judge if the People were ready to make their Opening Statement and she announced she was. At that moment, the Menendez trial began to a packed courtroom, almost four years after that fateful night. It had been decided that Lyle's jury would hear the Opening Statement first while Erik's jury waited outside the courtroom. The prosecutor stated how Lyle brutally shot his father six times with a shotgun and his mother was shot ten times. She said she would be calling witnesses to show how the brothers were 'lying in wait' to kill their parents when they were least expecting it. She listed the names of witnesses who would make their case.

The prosecution had only recently been told the defendants would be telling the jury a story of how they were in fear of their parents and had to kill them in self-defense. To counter the Defense, the prosecutor wanted the jury to see how frequently they told lies. She gave an example in which Lyle hired a bodyguard to protect him when he knew no was out to kill him. In other words, Lyle frequently lied and therefore he was lying about the child abuse the brothers had allegedly suffered at the hands of their parents.

She mentioned to the jury how Lyle had gone on a wild spending spree shortly after they killed their parents. She mentioned the purchases of Rolex watches, Marina apartments, a $60,000 Porsche, and a restaurant for $550,000.

After Prosecutor Bozanich was finished with her Opening Statement, it was then time for Lyle's attorney, Jill Lansing, to give her Opening Statement. She started out by saying, "We're not disputing **what happened**. The only thing you are going to have to focus on in this trial is **why it happened**."

"What we will prove to you is that the murders were committed out of fear. Fear of two parents who were so brutal, so manipulative, and so sexually perverse that they drove their own sons to the most desperate act of defilement."

She indicated the Defense would rely heavily on the testimony of experts in the field of child abuse, to give meaning and understanding as to why the defendants acted the way they did. She didn't spell out the details of what the various experts would testify to but asked the jury to carefully listen to their explanations. She suggested that her client, Lyle, would take the witness stand and explain why it had been necessary to kill their parents. The jurors had to wonder what she was really talking about, but they intently listened to her every word.

After finishing with Lyle's jury, they were excused and Erik's jury was called into the courtroom. Then it was time for the other Prosecutor, Lester Kuriyama, to give his Opening Statement regarding Erik. Lester was an experienced prosecutor of short stature. He had a buzz haircut that appeared to make him seem taller. He was soft-spoken and overly courteous. However, his demeanor changed when he was in the courtroom. His wording was always direct and concise. He didn't use weasel language but told it the way it was.

Sometimes the image of Lester was contrary to the strong words coming out of his mouth. He simplified the case into these few words: "The brothers wanted to execute their parents and they definitely didn't want to be caught." He explained how he would call Dr. Owens to testify to what Erik told him about the killing of his parents. The doctor would go on to relate how Erik and his brother went to San Diego and purchased the shotguns in the name of his brother's old roommate.

Prosecutor Kuriyama explained how Dr. Owens would tell how Erik thought Jose was too controlling of him and his brother. They believed their father was trying to disinherit them by changing his will to eliminate them as beneficiaries. The prosecutor said Erik had to kill his mother, Kitty, because she would have been a witness against them. Also, they believed that she would be miserable and suicidal without her husband, Jose.

He finished his Opening Statement by telling the jury the brothers tried to create a web of deception that included false alibis, lies to the police, using a stolen driver's license to purchase the murder weapons, and the hiring of a computer expert to delete computer files.

Then it was time for Erik's Defense Attorney, Leslie Abramson, to make her Opening Statement. Like a tornado cutting loose in the courtroom, she vigorously explained that Lyle had acted the way he did to defend his brother, Erik, who needed to be defended because he was the real victim in the family. She acknowledged Erik's revelation of abuse might look suspicious, especially after spending so much time in jail, before he revealed all the abuse he suffered as a child at the hands of his parents. The delay in telling about the abuse wasn't because it wasn't true but the feeling that no one would understand.

The real reason Erik didn't tell the truth earlier was that he did not trust Dr. Owens, or his best friend, Craig Curry, to understand what he had gone through. She assured the jurors they would hear from Erik, who would tell them why he had to kill his parents. She basically stated she would call numerous child abuse experts who would put everything in perspective.

CHAPTER 44 FIRST TRIAL—WITNESSES

After the Opening Statements, the judge took a recess, after which both juries were assembled in the courtroom so the actual trial could begin. The prosecution called the first witness, a police dispatcher, and the playing of the 9-1-1 tape, which was the starting point of when the police involvement was set in motion. The jurors listened closely to Lyle's voice describing how they had come home and were surprised to find their father and mother shot to death in the family room. They could hear how calm Lyle was compared to his brother, who appeared to be emotionally distraught.

The prosecution's purpose in playing this for the jurors was to show how devious the brothers were in pretending that someone else had shot their parents when now they were admitting to doing it. Officer Butkus was called as the next witness. He described how he had arrived at the house and shortly thereafter the two brothers ran out of the house yelling and falling on the lawn continually saying, "Oh my God." He claimed the brothers said that they had found their parents shot to death. At no time did either brother indicate they had to shoot their parents because they were afraid they were about to be killed by them.

Following the officer's testimony, the prosecutors called the captain of the fishing boat to testify that the family had gone deep sea fishing on the day before the shooting. He related how he found the family to be peculiar in that the father was doing all the fishing at the back of the boat while the brothers were huddled together at the front of the boat. Kitty was having problems with seasickness, and the brothers weren't doing any fishing; all they did was talk to each other for the seven hours they were at sea. The captain indicated that in his experience, most families fish and interact with each other, but not the Menendez family.

On cross-examination, the Defense attorneys tried to bring out that the brothers could have thought they were about to be killed while out at sea. But the strange part of that suggestion was that numerous staff members were on the boat and would have been witnesses if their parents had tried to kill the boys at sea.

Det. Zoeller was the next witness called to testify. He related that he examined the crime scene to see if he could figure out the reason for the shooting. It didn't appear to be a burglary or home invasion robbery. What he found was the brothers had come back at 5:30 a.m. and asked the officers outside if they could go into the house to retrieve their tennis rackets because they had a game later that day. Det. Zoeller told them no, they would have to wait until the Coroner had completed their investigation and removed the bodies.

After Det. Zoeller had finished his direct testimony, it was time for cross-examination by Lesley Abramson, who asked about whether he had noticed any animal droppings. This set the witness back, wondering what animal droppings had to do with this case. He answered that he didn't see any. That was followed by how carefully did he look for dog feces? He had to admit he didn't look for any animal droppings. Lesley was trying to plant a seed that Kitty Menendez was a poor housekeeper and likewise a poor mother.

An additional detective was called, Sgt. Edmonds, who testified he became suspicious when Erik said that when they entered house he could smell smoke. The sergeant couldn't understand how the brothers could smell smoke. If there had been a smell of smoke, it had to be close to the time of the shooting, and since some windows had been broken the smoke would have dissipated quickly.

The next witness would continue to be questioned in regards to the smoke issue after the firing of the Mossberg shotguns. This witness, Deputy Fiorarms, was qualified as an expert witness dealing with firearms. He discounted the smell of smoke; however, the issue was now moot since the brothers were admitting to shooting the shotguns. Most of this witness's testimony involved the operation of the Mossberg shotguns. The prosecutors wanted to show the various acts one had to go through to fire this type of shotgun. In particular, the shooter has to do two separate pumps in order to shoot an additional round. They wanted to show there was an act of premeditation between each shot. In other words, the shooter had to go through numerous acts to fire the weapon. One doesn't accidentally fire numerous rounds from a Mossberg shotgun.

Lyle's friend Perry Bryan (pseudonym) was the next witness called to show how the defendants were trying to use him to establish an alibi that they were together. Since the defendants were now admitting to the shooting, they really didn't need an alibi, but it did show how devious they were.

The next witness was Erik's friend Craig Curry, who gave a chilling account of what happened on the night of the shooting. He testified before Erik's jury that 12 days after the shooting he was visiting Erik at the Menendez house when Erik said,

"This is what happened." He walked him through every step, all of the way into the family room where they shot their parents. At no time did Erik mention anything about sexual or any other type of abuse.

The prosecutors wanted to ask Craig about a screenplay titled ***Friends*** that he and Erik wrote when they were 16 years old. The story was about sons who learned their parents had taken out a large life insurance policy and made their sons the beneficiaries. The sons decided to kill their parents so they could get all the inheritance as quickly as possible. Obviously, the prosecutors couldn't have a better example at Erik's state of mind, since it almost parroted the entire killing of Jose and Kitty. His Defense Attorney, Lesley Abramson, vehemently objected, claiming this was mere fiction that had been written several years before the crime. The judge was persuaded by the remoteness argument and the prosecutors were precluded from mentioning anything about this screenplay.

The next witness was Donovan Guthman, who testified he had been a dorm mate of Lyle's back at Princeton. He related how he had been accused of taking some items and was told to move out of the dorm quickly. In his rush to get out, he left his wallet with his California driver's license and other identification behind. He testified he didn't purchase two Mossberg shotguns in San Diego. The prosecutors then asked him if he had ever talked to Lyle about child abuse issues. He said he opened up to Lyle about how he had been abused as a child. Lyle at no time mentioned anything about being abused himself.

On cross-examination, Donovan was asked if he ever told a reporter he had heard about Jose molesting Lyle. He said he hadn't heard that as a fact but there were some rumors going around. Glen Stone was called next by the prosecution. He was a close friend of Lyle and was with him during much of the spending spree. Glen was also present when Donovan's wallet was found by Lyle. Glen stated, "Lyle held on to it. He told me about a new will and he was getting someone to erase that new will from the computer." He was also with Lyle when he flew to Los Angeles when Lyle heard the police were looking for him at Princeton. Lyle gave Glen money to bail him out, as well as a business card with contact information for attorney Gerald Chaleff. Lyle told him about Dr. Owens's tapes and said, "If the police get their hands on those tapes, I'm fucked." Since Glen Stone testified to some incriminating facts about Lyle, the Defense tried to make him out as a liar since he had done some puffing-up on his resume that the Defense attorney had discovered in their investigation.

Prosecutors then called Dr. Irwin Gordon (pseudonym), the Coroner Medical Examiner. Some jurors in homicide cases look forward to the coroner's testifying about conducting the autopsy, because they have a ghoulish side to their personality. However, there are just as many jurors who cringe at the thought of listening to the coroner. Everyone has an image of a mortician as an older man in a black suit, with a pasty complexion and a thinning hairline with a grave expressionless face. What would be the stereotype of a coroner? Dr. Gordon projects the image of a coroner. For years he has worn the same out-of-date sports coat with wide lapels and the same faded gray pants. His fashion accent was a god-awful tie that could only be found in a thrift store. What is so disarming about him is the fact that he is always smiling, as though he enjoys his job of sawing up bodies and snipping out various body parts.

Dr. Gordon wasn't the star witness in this case since no one had any questions as to the cause or time of death. He testified that the male, Jose Menendez, had been shot six times, and the female, Kitty Menendez, had suffered ten shotgun wounds, several of which were birdshot. From his examination, he concluded they had been shot in succession but couldn't give an opinion as the order of the shots. The prosecutors had to be careful as to what coroner photos they should show the jury since most of the photos were so ghastly that they were not ready for prime time showing.

By August 4 the prosecution was ready for their star witness, Dr. Owens. The judge had ruled the psychiatrist couldn't use the word "sociopath" to describe the brothers. The judge believed it was a word that had various meanings and wasn't a medical term. Dr. Owens testified before both juries that the brothers wanted to kill Jose because he was dominating their lives and made them feel inferior. Kitty was killed because they didn't want her to be a witness who could testify against them. Erik said that Jose had planned to disinherit them, which was also another reason for killing him. Dr. Owens also testified that Erik told him the plan to kill Jose and Kitty was conceived when Erik was been watching the **Billionaire Boys Club** TV mini-series. Although the prosecution was restricted as to what occurred in their first session, Dr. Owens testified to each of the brother's explanation as to why and how they had killed their parents. He also related how Lyle had threatened him if he told the police about anything they had told him.

The Defense was waiting to have a chance to attack Dr. Owens. On cross-examination they brought up the fact that he was having an affair with a former patient, Jordan Shay, and had improperly prescribed drugs for her. Finally, they got him to admit he had paid $400,000.00 to Ms. Shay in a civil court settlement.

At the end of the prosecution's case, Lester tried to have a copy of the Billionaire Boys Club (BBC) TV mini-series placed into evidence to be shown later to the juries, as it was the blueprint on how to commit the perfect murder. However, the judge listened to the Defense's objections and ruled that it was not admissible. This seemed to be a strange ruling, since the brothers were planning to testify that it was the watching of this TV mini-series where they got the idea to murder their parents.

CHAPTER 45 DEFENSE PRESENTED IN FIRST TRIAL

The prosecution had done their job of proving that Lyle and Erik Menendez both shot and killed their parents, Jose and Kitty. No one in the courtroom had any doubt what the brothers had done. Now the job of the Defense was to turn everything upside down so the juries believed that the brothers were justified in what they did. In order for the brothers to go completely free, the Defense had to show the brothers believed they were in imminent danger before they killed their parents. The Defense needed to prove two things: one, that Lyle and Erik had been in fear of their lives and two, the conduct of their parents would have produced the same belief in a 'reasonable person's' mind.

This latter requirement was such a high hurdle for the Defense. How could they possibly say, with a straight face, that a 'reasonable person' would have such a state of mind? The judge recognized that he would have to allow a wide range of witnesses in order to prove that state of mind.

The Defense started by having Lyle testify. He was on the witness stand for nine days. The story began several days before the shooting, when Lyle and his mother got into a screaming match after Kitty allegedly reached for Lyle's hair and grabbed and pulled on it. All of a sudden, Lyle's toupee came off his head. He had worn a hairpiece for a number of years, ever since he had started losing his hair when he was around 14 years of age. According to the story, this shocked Erik, who claimed he was unaware his brother wore a toupee. After this incident, when the brothers were alone, Erik confided in Lyle how sorry he felt for the humiliation it must have caused him. Erik started complaining about both of their parents and began relating how their dad had been molesting him for years.

At that point, Lyle claimed he opened up and told Erik about the molestation he had endured as a young child. Then Lyle said he was going to put a stop to this abuse of Erik. Shortly thereafter, Lyle confronted their father and told him to stop molesting Erik. Lyle said that Jose didn't deny it but only said he would do whatever he wanted to do since this was his family. Lyle threaten his father by saying if he didn't stop molesting Erik, he was going to tell everyone he was a child molester. Lyle said his father threatened him back if he ever told anyone.

So that was the chronology of events that led to the fear that Jose was about to kill both of them, to make sure they never told anyone about the molestation. Lyle was asked by his attorney to explain about the sexual abuse to him. Lyle said that the molestation occurred between the ages of six to eight. When he was 13, he believed his father was molesting his brother Erik. Lyle then added to the abuse by claiming his mother sexually abused him when he was 12 by letting him touch her all over her body.

However, his attorney knew this was a tall tail for the jury to accept so she started asking the questions the jurors would want to know. She asked, "If it was so bad, why didn't you run away?" Lyle's response was he knew his father was so powerful he would make him come back. The next question was, why didn't he go to the police? His response was that they wouldn't believe him.

His attorney knew that the prosecutors would hit hard in certain areas, and she wanted to soften the blow by giving Lyle an opportunity to spin the comment in his favorite. The Defense was aware that the prosecution was ready to call Lyle's former girlfriend, Jamie Pincus (pseudonym), to testify that Lyle had asked her to come to court and testify that Jose had made unwanted sexual advances toward her. By the Defense asking him first, he could explain that he did it out of desperation.

The prosecution questioned Lyle as to why he hadn't told Dr. Owens about the sexual abuse by his father, Jose. Lyle was able to explain by saying he didn't trust Dr. Owens. Lyle went on to criticize Dr. Owens. He said he had never bragged that he had committed the perfect murder. Lyle's attorney, Jill Lansing, did an admirable job of having Lyle weave a web of sexual abuse and by totally destroying the decent reputations of Jose and Kitty Menendez.

Prosecutor Pam Bozanich was taking notes of every allegation Lyle made while testifying. Pam was bright, with a good memory, and she didn't miss anything he said. For four days she continued to cross-examine him, catching him in numerous inconsistencies. If Lyle was being tried for being a liar, he definitely would be found guilty. Over the past five years, Lyle had explained various facts differently to other people.

When Pam pressed him if there had been any actual threats made by his parents, he had to admit there were none. As to the question if his father had any guns, he had to admit he knew of none. Near the end of the cross-examination, Pam looked at him and stated that his story didn't make much sense, Lyle agreed. During all four days of cross-examination, Lyle was able to control his emotions. He would cry when it was appropriate to cry. He seemed to get better with his answers the longer he sat on the witness stand. Some thought Lyle came across as being too well rehearsed. The testimony was lengthy and very intense. It was time for his little brother to take his place in the witness chair. Everyone in the courtroom wondered how well would Erik do as a witness. Could Erik do as well as his big brother when testifying before the jury?

CHAPTER 46 ERIK TAKES THE WITNESS STAND

On September 27, Erik went up to the witness stand and raised his right hand and took an oath to 'tell nothing but the whole truth.' Erik had a much gentler personality and wasn't as confident as his brother. He had watched his brother testify and noticed even his big brother had difficulties keeping his story straight. Nonetheless, his brother was sharp enough to know how to fend off the tough questions.

Erik's demeanor wasn't helping him, since he looked awkward as he gazed out at the spectators and news media with his small, beady eyes. Some might think he looked deranged, or like a deer caught in the glare of headlights. His attorney, Leslie Abramson, knew what was at stake and had been working for years to craft the evidence to fit their story. Leslie wanted to protect him since he was the weakest link to their case. She moved the attorney's lectern, which originally was behind the counsel table, to be closer to the witness box. In that way she could be closer to her client in order to provide moral support.

So began the easy questions by his attorney. However, Erik was no rocket scientist, and even with the questions they had gone over for years, he still struggled to keep his answers straight. He was asked about his mother and explained to the jury that he thought she had magical powers because she seemed to know everything about him. He talked about how his father had molested him over the years. He was able to relate the same story Lyle had given regarding how his mother had pulled Lyle's toupee off, which shocked him, since he didn't know that his big brother wore a hairpiece. That was when he first told his brother about the abuse he had suffered at the hands of his father.

Erik may have been proud of his ability to tell the story without tripping up. Yet for some reason he wanted to share with the jury more than they wanted to know. He volunteered the following information to paint the most despicable picture of his father. He said he had heard, through some of his friends, that by putting cinnamon in his father's tea or coffee it would make the the semen tastier. As some of the jurors tried to digest that thought, others flinched and recoiled in their seats.

Leslie tried to keep Erik on track, but at times he strayed from the script and his attorney, at times, treated him like a hostile witness trying to get him to provide direct answers and stop him from volunteering. Erik tried to cry on cue, but sometimes he misplaced his emotions. He and his attorney seemed to tell their story to jurors, which made him look like a young teenager floundering around. The direct examination was over and now he had to be confronted with the tougher questions.

Prosecutor Lester Kuriyama had a long list of questions he wanted to ask Erik. There were a number of inconsistencies in Erik's story, and Lester was going to give him a chance to explain them away. It had been almost five years since the shootings, and Erik was having difficulty keeping his stories straight.

Lester asked Erik about his testimony where he and his brother had looked at two handguns at the Big 5 Sporting Goods store in Santa Monica on the Friday before the shooting. They were told that there would be a 15-day waiting period for handguns. They didn't want to wait that long so they left and went to San Diego, where they were able to buy the shotguns immediately. Lester wanted Erik to make sure he understood the question. Erik listened carefully and responded that he was absolutely sure they had looked at handguns at the Big 5 in Santa Monica.

Lester then casually asked if he knew that the Big 5 store in Santa Monica had stopped carrying and selling handguns at that store two years prior to the shooting. At that moment, Erik's face had the look of "Oh Shit, how do I get out of this?" The prosecution was going to have a manager from the store come into court to testify that the store, at the time of the shooting, was not in possession of hand guns or selling them. Yet Erik's only response was they still showed him handguns.

Next, the prosecutor asked Erik if he had seen the Billionaire Boys Club mini-series, to which he responded he had never seen it. This seemed a strange answer since he had told so many people that he and his brother had watched the mini-series on TV and that was where they had conceived the idea of killing their parents.

Erik was not faring well under cross-examination and drifted into answering that he was having difficulty remembering any details. When pressed about the possibility his parents were about to disinherit him and his brother, his response was that he never thought they would actually change their will. This was contrary to what he had told so many of his friends.

The prosecutor was trying to bring in the fact that Erik was gay, which would explain certain things around the house. However, the judge, out of the presence of the jury, ruled there could not be any testimony about Erik's sexuality. The prosecution didn't think it was fair for the Defense to mention that there were gay porn magazines in the Menendez house. The inference was that Jose was the one who brought them into the house for his own enjoyment. This would be a form of corroborating the Defense position that Jose was committing homosexual acts on his sons.

The prosecution argued that by showing that Erik was gay, the inference was that he could be the source of the gay magazines. However, the judge would not permit any evidence as to Erik's sexuality, even if the jurors misconstrued who was the source of the gay magazines in the house.

CHAPTER 47 DEFENSE EXPERTS

The cross-examination of the brothers was one of the highlight of the trial, but now it was time to permit the Defense to bring in their expert witnesses to support the brothers' testimony. Thousands of dollars had been spent on finding individuals who would be willing, for the right amount of money, to say things that would help the brothers in their Defense. The Defense called their first expert to the witness stand, Ann Tyler, a Salt Lake City psychologist, who testified that both brothers suffered from "learned helplessness." She indicated this condition is the result of intense repeated abuse. She was vigorously cross-examined by the prosecution since there had been no corroboration of the sexual abuse as the brothers' claimed they suffered. How "learned helplessness" applied to rich kids in Beverly Hills was not clearly understood, but this expert witness claimed this condition was not easily faked.

The next Defense expert was Ann Burgess, a professor of psychiatric mental health nursing at the University of Pennsylvania. She also held herself out to be an expert in crime scene analysis. She said that the crime scene was disorganized and could not have been the product of a premeditated murder. She testified she spent considerable time reviewing all the photos of the interior of the house. She also claimed certain areas of the house appeared to be messy. It wasn't clear what she was referring to by that statement. Was the messiness due to the police searching for evidence of a Burglary or Robbery? When she looked at the photos of the victims' bodies, she noticed random wounds that led her to believe there was an overkill element, which showed a lack planning. What this all meant was escaping the comprehension of most everyone in the courtroom. Lyle's attorney called Stuart Hart, a professor from the University of Indiana who believed Lyle had been mistreated, psychologically by his father. It wasn't clear what that was based on, but this mistreatment continued for a considerable amount of time and left psychological scars on Lyle.

The next witness was Jon Conte. He had interviewed Lyle for 560 hours in 1993 and believed Lyle was telling the truth about the abuse because of the effect it had on him. This witness apparently was supposed to explain why Lyle and Erik hadn't immediately reported the abuse to Dr. Owens or to the police. This witness said Lyle suffered from shame and was reluctant to talk about the abuse because it was embarrassing for him to explain the various sexual acts he claimed had been perpetrated on him by his father.

The Defense knew that they had an uphill battle to sell the jury on the abuse, especially since there wasn't any corroboration. Their next witness was Dr. Kerry English, the medical director of the child abuse team at Martin Luther King Hospital, who would show in his testimony there was some corroboration. Dr. English had examined Erik for evidence of sodomy. After he had performed a thorough examine, he said he found no evidence of scarring or marks in his rectum to show he had suffered from sodomizing. However, when Dr. English was reviewing Erik's medical records, he found mention of "hurt posterior pharynx, uvula, and soft palate healing well." He testified to the jury that could have been caused by oral copulation. He went on to explain that if a large penis continuously rammed against that part of young person's throat it could cause such an injury.

On cross-examination he admitted there were many other possibilities as to what could cause this type injury, such as a popsicle stick or any eating utensil. By this time it wasn't clear whether some jurors were disgusted, or wondering if things could get any weirder.

What happened next in the court was a big surprise. The Defense had fought for years to make sure that the jurors never heard the tapes of the brothers confessing to Dr. Owens. Then unexpectedly, the Defense played for the jury Dr. Owens's tape of December 11 with the brothers' voices explaining what they had done. The judge made the brothers and counsel waive forever any patient-therapist privilege. The Defense wanted the jury to hear the fear in the brothers' voices.

On the tape, Lyle bragged that he and Erik had shown great courage in killing their mother. Lyle said, "I miss not having my parents around, just like I miss not having my dog around. If I can make such a gross analogy?" However, nowhere on the tape does either brother mention any sexual abuse, only that Jose had to be killed because he was too controlling of the brothers' lives, as well as he was a bad husband.

What was also unusual was the fact the Defense called Jordan Shay to discredit Dr. Owens by showing that he was a manipulator and had bullied her during their relationship. This witness was changing her testimony from what she had first told the detectives about overhearing what the brothers had said in their sessions. She denied any statements she had made to the police. She claimed she had been brainwashed by Dr. Owens into saying the things she had stated earlier. Her testimony was confusing at best.

The court watchers wondered what had changed her from a strong prosecution witness to a Defense witness. Apparently, the wrath of the psychiatrist's girlfriend was directed toward the DA's Office for **not filing rape charges against Dr. Owens**. This was her way of getting back at the DA's Office by changing her testimony in order to hurt the prosecution. Often the DA's Office finds itself in a 'No Win' situation. Here, the police and DA's Office were highly indebted to Dr. Owens and Jordan Shay. If Dr. Owens hadn't recorded the brothers and hadn't asked his girlfriend to listen in, the brothers would very likely be roaming freely among us. To carry that logic even further, if Dr. Owens hadn't been such an ass in dumping Jordan, she never would have been motivated to go to the police. Thankfully, they did what they did, but that wasn't grounds for the DA's Office to file criminal charges against the psychiatrist to placate the ex-girlfriend.

There seems to be some kind of pattern in all this. When this type of girlfriend wants to get even with someone who hasn't given her what she wants, she strikes back in overkill mode. With Dr. Owens, when she revealed the tapes, she had to know it would cause him to lose his Psychiatrist License. With the DA's Office, she switched sides when she didn't get her way with filing rape charges against the 'good doctor.'

The DA's Office had gone out of their way to have independent prosecutors review the police reports on the alleged rape. What it turned out to be was her word against his. Those prosecutors looked for corroboration of her claims but could not find any. What it all looked like was a psychiatrist who unethically took advantage of an attractive redhead who consented to sexual activities. How vulnerable was she?

We will never know for sure. What we do know is, she is one lady you don't want to cross unless you are willing to pay dearly. (For starters, Dr. Owens paid dearly by losing his psychiatrist license and paying her a civil settlement of $400,000.)

CHAPTER 48 REBUTTAL

After the Defense had put on their case, which included both defendants and all the expert witnesses, the DA had to reassess their strategy as to how to present their case to the two juries. First, they had to contradict the stories told by the brothers about the days leading up to the murders. Second, they had to try and rehabilitate the reputations of both Jose and Kitty. This was a daunting task for the prosecution.

The prosecution's first rebuttal witness was Grant Williams (pseudonym), the pool cleaner. Most likely only in his wildest dreams would a pool cleaner ever think he would be on national TV, testifying to what he overheard while trying to fix an automatic spa control valve. He testified that he was called out on the Saturday before the murders to work on the pool. While trying to make the adjustments on the pool equipment, he saw Lyle playing tennis and Jose and Kitty eating on the patio next to the tennis court. It seemed to the witness that Lyle was angry about his game and Erik was angry about something else. The reason the prosecution put this witness on was because the brothers had testified earlier, before the jury, they were afraid of their parents and were trying to stay as far away from them as possible, but there they were, in their parents' presence.

The next rebuttal witness was Flora Silva (pseudonym), the Menendez family housekeeper. She worked and stayed at the house Monday through Friday. She said she never heard Kitty or Jose yelling at either one of the brothers. She was asked about the Tuesday before the shooting and whether she ever overheard Lyle crying when his toupee was allegedly pulled off by his mother. She said she hadn't seen any fighting or arguments between any members of the Menendez family.

The Defense had anticipated Lyle's former girlfriend, Jamie Pincus, would be called to testify regarding Lyle asking her to lie about Jose making sexual advances towards her. However, now the prosecution was using her to testify that she was with Lyle when he got a toupee in Birmingham, Alabama. She remembered she had had a conversation about Lyle's hairpiece with Erik way back in 1988. In other words, when Erik claimed he didn't know his big brother wore a hairpiece until 1989, he was lying or mistaken.

It was hard for the prosecution to know what witnesses to call to try and rehabilitate Jose and Kitty's reputation as parents. The DA called Brian Andersen, Kitty's brother. He said that Jose had not abused either one of his sons. Nevertheless, Jose had said to him that Lyle had to learn to support himself. He admitted Jose was disappointed by the lack of responsibility that either boy showed.

The prosecution was grasping for anyone who could provide insight into how Jose and Kitty were as parents. Next, the DA called Marlene Ehrlich (pseudonym), Jose's secretary for 14 years. She had seen the interrelationship of the family and knew there were disappointments in the sons' behavior. As parents, they just wanted the best for their children. Marlene remembered when the brothers were in the limo with her and traveling back from the memorial service in New Jersey. Lyle asked, "Who said I couldn't fill my father's shoes?" Marlene thought she would give him some advice by saying, "Make your own tracks in life and don't try to fill your dad's shoes." Lyle immediately replied, "You don't understand, these are my father's shoes."

The DA finished off their Rebuttal without calling any child abuse experts. Pam Bozanich reflected on all the Defense experts who never seemed to hit the bull's-eye of the Defense's theory of the case. The DA had a child abuse expert who sat through the testimony of most of the Defense experts and Pam didn't see where she needed to turn this trial into a battle of the experts. The prosecutor was afraid if she called her own expert witnesses, the jurors would think that she was giving the Defense some credibility. Pam had talked to other prosecutors who indicated that the Defense experts had not been effective. At the end of the Rebuttal, Pam thought long and hard and couldn't imagine any of the jurors would be so naïve as to give any credence to the numerous Defense experts.

The Defense had more witnesses for their Surrebuttal. (In an adversarial process, for instance, a court proceeding, a **surrebuttal** is a response to the opposing party's rebuttal; in essence it is a rebuttal to a rebuttal.) Dr. Vega (pseudonym), who had interviewed Erik extensively, was called as an additional witness to support the validity of the abuse, and classified Erik as being a basket case from all the abuse he had allegedly endured. The Defense also called Mark Hadley (pseudonym), the tennis coach who claimed he was with the brothers on August 19, the day before the shooting. This was to counter the pool man's testimony that he saw the brothers with their parents in the backyard.

Now it was up to the jurors to decide whom to believe. The judge had to make some preliminary rulings in order for the attorneys to prepare their Arguments. The judge declined to give the jury any instructions that could lead to an acquittal. The judge said there was simply no evidence that an **average person** would have been in fear for his or her life, as the brothers described the events that occurred on that date. That was big for the prosecution, since it meant the brothers most likely were not going to walk out as free men. The Defense knew this would be hard to convince the jury and it was wishful thinking on the part of the defendants.

CHAPTER 49 ARGUMENT AND DELIBERATIONS

This trial had been strenuous and stressful since it lasted longer than anticipated. Everyone was ready for it to be over. When it was announced that Argument was about to commence, everyone sighed with relief. Pam, the prosecutor, was ready to argue before Lyle's jury. The question was, how do you want the jurors to approach the case? Even though the case took months to try, Pam wanted the jurors to look at it as a simple case. The victims were watching TV in their family room when their sons came in and slaughtered them. To prove premeditation, all the jurors had to do was look at the fact they both drove to San Diego, several days in advance, to purchase the shotguns they used to kill their parents with.

Pam didn't mince words in her description of the brothers. She said, "Lyle and Erik are nothing but spoiled vicious brats who got the best Defense daddy's money could buy." For a lot of children who have been severely abused and still have become useful members of society, this defense is an offense. She seemed to be expressing what a lot of members of the public believed as they watched the trial on TV. She didn't need to argue to the public, she needed to persuade Lyle's jurors. They had been bombarded for weeks by the defense experts, who had tried to provide some type of explanation for the brothers' conduct.

Next up was the Defense Attorney, Michael Burt, telling Lyle's jurors they must consider the murders were carried out while the brothers were in a state of fear and panic followed by years of abuse by bullying parents. He claimed Lyle operated as an unthinking robot as he shot his parents on instinct, not as a carefully thought out plan. This wasn't first degree murder but something far less. Jill Lansing, Lyle's other attorney, walked the jurors through the crime and asked them to consider all the events dating back to Lyle's childhood when he was sexually molested. It wasn't clear what they were asking the jurors to do, but it certainly wasn't a first degree murder case.

Then it was time to argue in Erik's case. Prosecutor Lester Kuryama began by stating that the prosecution had proved that Erik was involved in his parents' murder. Lester argued for three hours and asked the jurors to use their common sense in deciding the case. He walked the jurors through the actions of the brothers in the planning and carrying out the shooting. He dismissed the Defense experts for not proving anything that would justify the brothers' belief that they were under an imminent threat of death. Their parents had done nothing to make threats against the brothers. If the brothers were in so much fear, why were they playing tennis in the presence of their parents? Also, why would they go with their parents on a seven-hour fishing trip the day before if they felt so frightened by their parents?

It was time now for Erik's attorney, Leslie Abramson, to commence her marathon three-day Argument. She went over every detail of the case from start to finish. She didn't want to miss one point, no matter how relevant or irrelevant it was. It seemed she was throwing everything against the wall in hopes something would stick in the mind of at least one juror. The theme of her Argument was that all of the DA's witnesses were liars and you couldn't believe a thing they said. But she seemed to save her most deadly venom for Dr. Owens. She thought of him as a mere toadstool, like something to kick over. She despised everything about him, and anytime she could berate him she would. Leslie might have thought if only Dr. Owens hadn't two-timed his girlfriend she would never have gone to the police.

Everyone was surprised when Leslie broke ranks with Lyle and his attorneys. She told the jurors, "I don't want Erik to take the rap for Lyle. The evidence in this case does not prove that Erik killed anybody. Most of the testimony showed that it was Lyle who snuck into the family room and fired first at Jose and later Kitty. It was never clear how much shooting Erik actually did." One argument could be made that Lyle did all the shooting, actually killing the victims, and Erik's later shooting occurred after Kitty had already expired. The most that Erik would be guilty of was mutilating a corpse, (if Kitty had been already killed by Lyle).

The Arguments by the prosecution and Defense were over and the tedious jury instructions were read. Basically, the judge gave both juries four choices:

Could be guilty or not guilty of First Degree Murder

Could be guilty or not guilty of Second Degree Murder

Could be guilty or not guilty of Voluntary Manslaughter

Could be guilty or not guilty of Involuntary Manslaughter

Erik's jury deliberated 16 days and was unable to reach an agreement on any of the counts. Lyle's jury deliberated for 24 days and was hopelessly deadlocked. In both cases, the judge declared a mistrial and the cases were set for a new trial date. The new District Attorney, Gil Garcetti, immediately announced the two brothers would be re-tried. Some reporters from the news media praised the Defense for carefully rehearsing the testimony with their witnesses. On the other hand, the media criticized the prosecutors for letting the case get away from them. The media also faulted the judge for being indecisive and making some questionable legal rulings. Others from the media claimed the jurors were too gullible in accepting such an outlandish Defense.

CHAPTER 50 THE SECOND TRIAL—DA'S CASE

Two and half years had elapsed between the first and second trial of the brothers. During that hiatus, the public was subjected to the O. J. Simpson trial, which was billed as ***'the greatest trial of the century.'*** That case consumed the attention of the news media, illustrating how gavel-to-gavel TV coverage can turn a serious homicide trial into a TV frenzy. The Los Angeles DA's Office was highly criticized for permitting the case to spin out of control. By the time the second Menendez trial was commencing, everyone was gun-shy about gavel-to-gavel TV coverage. The judge and others had etched into their memories the circus-like atmosphere created by the TV coverage in the O. J. Simpson case.

This time Judge Stan Weisberg said, "The TV coverage can increase the risk that jurors would be exposed to information and commentary about the case outside of the courtroom." This was a nice way to sidestep the news media's request for coverage. The first trial had taught the judge the problems that are encountered when trying to conduct a trial with two separate juries. The judge recognized the possible conflict in regard to statements made by one defendant implicating the other defendant. However, the judge said he would try to work around those problems in order to have only one jury.

The most important differences between the first and second trial was the fact that the Defense wouldn't be able to present experts to discuss the possibility of sexual abuse and its impact on the brothers' state of mind. In a pretrial hearing, the prosecution presented a line of appellate opinions that stated that claims of abuse couldn't be presented to the jury without evidence to substantiate such a claim. In the first trial, there was no evidence presented of child abuse except from the two defendants when they testified. If the Defense didn't come up with hard evidence as to child abuse, then those experts could not testify. In other words, this message to the Defense was, either call your witnesses or shut up.

The other big factor between the two trials was Lyle's ability to take the witness stand and spin his story about the sexual abuse. Lyle had done something every Defense attorney warns their clients not to do. That warning is to keep their mouths shut and don't say anything to damage their Defense. Lyle was the brother who would be described as the confident, if not cocky, one. He wasn't afraid of what was going on around him. His attorney subsequently told him he would not be able to take the witness stand in the second trial. What had Lyle done that prevented him from telling the jury his story that his dad was a child molester?

The answer was that Lyle was in constant contact with Norma Nison (pseudonym), who befriended the Menendez brothers between1991 to 1994. Over the years, Lyle had suggested he and Norma could write a book about his life in and out of jail. She tried to write down stories that Lyle told her. However, she couldn't write fast enough and asked him if she could record what he was saying. He said OK, so she let the tapes roll while talking to him over the phone from the jail. On one of the recordings, he said the following:

"I can't honestly say now that I felt that they (parents) were actually going to do something at that moment because now I know that they didn't have any weapons with them.

I can move a jury, I think. I get very emotional...I just affect people more. I can affect people in a very negative way, sometimes. Affect them in a very positive way."

She decided to work with the publisher, Dove, to write the book, ***The Private Diary of Lyle Menendez: In His Own Words***, for which she was paid an advance of $12,500. Part of the deal was to sell the tapes to the publisher. From that point on they were in the public domain and available to the DA's Office.

Once the prosecution obtained a copy of the tapes, they decided to use them in the second trial if, in fact, Lyle decided to testify. The best way to describe Lyle's situation was **CHECKMATE.** You could almost hear Lyle humming Cher's hit tune from 1989, ***If I Could Turn Back Time.***

There wasn't anything worse for the Defense, since Lyle was the better witness between the two brothers. He was smart, focused, and could remember what he needed to say to tell the abuse story to the jury.

Another major factor that was making the second Menendez trial completely different was due to the attorneys involved in the case. Pam Bozanich, who had been the lead prosecutor in the first trial, stepped down after receiving criticism for the manner in which she had tried the case. She had been one of the brightest and toughest prosecutors in the DA's Office, with a wealth of experience in grisly homicide cases. She was the victim of what happens when the Defense attorneys play games with the prosecution by not turning over Discovery to the prosecutor in a timely fashion. She didn't have sufficient time to prepare for the last minute Defense they had sprung on her.

At the beginning of the first trial, the Defense provided no names of witnesses or reports to the prosecution as to all these child abuse and sexual abuse experts they were planning to call as witnesses. It was only at the last minute, just weeks before the trial, that Pam discovered the Defense wasn't going to change from 'we didn't do it' to 'we did it because we thought our parents were going to kill us.' There was no way Pam could have anticipated that the Defense would include all these experts who would claim these defendants had been so abused by their parents they were acting like human robots.

The strong criticism the media had flung at Pam for not reacting fast enough to the changing course of the Defense could be argued as to whether or not it was fair. The old adage, 'you don't change horses in mid-stream' didn't apply to this situation, in which the DA's Office found itself in the middle of two trials and needed to replace the prosecutors. It was decided they would assign the acting head deputy of Major Crimes Division, David Conn, and put him in charge of the Menendez case.

David Conn was by far the most knowledgeable attorney regarding homicide trials and homicide law. David had been trying cases for 18 years and had become an incredibly proficient attorney and a consummate litigator. He definitely was a detail person and knew the law so well that judges relied on him to provide them with the most up-to-date case law. When he tried a case, the court watchers, law clerks, and even new attorneys packed the courtrooms to watch him in action during a trial.

What mesmerized all those watching was the fact that David projected the appearance of Clark Kent, aka Superman, with his glasses and his impeccable suits.

This image didn't go unnoticed by jurors. He was more than a comic character. During the Vietnam War he was a Marine and had accrued a toughness which was more of a resolve that every battle could be won with preparation and a tactical approach. David was a fierce contender.

CHAPTER 51 NEW APPROACH TO CASE

Then David took over the case, he read the transcripts of the first trial frontward and backward, analyzing every move made by the Defense as he tried to develop a new approach to the case. First, David and his co-prosecutor, Carol Najera, spent weeks in the law library researching ways to block the brothers from presenting a 'Battered Person's Syndrome Defense.' From their research, David was able to put together a legal brief proving to the judge that child abuse can't be claimed without hard evidence proving its existence. David argued his motion before the judge. He showed how the appellate authority didn't support the judge's original ruling from the first trial. The judge was convinced of his error and reversed his ruling and stated that the Defense could only use the 'Battered Person's Syndrome' if they had corroborating evidence of its existence.

This reversal for the Defense meant their child abuse experts weren't going to be allowed to testify. The DA's Office hired Dr. Park Elliot Dietz, a well-known forensic psychiatrist, to assist them in knowing how to attack any mental Defense they might present. In the first trial, the prosecutor thought none of the jurors would be so naïve as to give credence to the myriad of Defense experts that the Defense called.

This time the DA was going to have an expert ready to testify against the Defense, if it became necessary.

Prosecutor David Conn gave considerable thought whether to call as witness Dr. Owens, as well as his former girlfriend. When David read over the first trial transcript, he saw how the Defense was able to ferociously attack both witnesses. The Defense made Dr. Owens look like the most unethical psychiatrist to ever walk the face of the earth. His former girlfriend was outright hostile to the DA's Office for not filing rape charges against the good doctor. These two witnesses were problematic for the prosecution. Their presence gave the Defense an opportunity to attack the DA's witnesses as being shady, sleazy, and slimy. David was a strategic thinker who realized the Defense had waived their right regarding the therapist-client privilege since they used the tapes in the first trial. So David came up with the idea of merely playing the tape of the two brothers confessing to the shooting of their parents. Years earlier, the California Supreme Court had ruled that the DA could use such a tape before the jury when privilege had been waived. This was a brilliant strategy in getting the tapes before the jury without having to call either Dr. Owens or his former girlfriend.

The prosecutors, David Conn and his assistant Carol Najera, had two and half years to figure out ways to avoid the pitfalls of the first trial. However, the Defense attorneys had changed slightly. By the time of the second trial, the Menendez brothers claimed they were indigent and the court was required to pay for their Defense. All the money they were supposed to inherit was diverted to other relatives. The court was required to appoint attorneys to represent them, at taxpayers' expense. Leslie Abramson was able to talk the judge into appointing her to continue representing Erik. She was assisted by Barry Levin. However, in Lyle's case, Jill

Lansing was not assigned to represent him, but was substituted with the Public Defender's Office. To represent Lyle, they brought in Charles Gessler, the dean of Death Penalty defenses, to be assisted by Terri Towery.

Judge Weisberg had learned from the first trial how a case can mushroom out of control. To prevent that from reoccurring, he limited the Defense to 64 witnesses, compared to the 101 witnesses in the first trial. (The second trial lasted for only 23 weeks.) Jury selection started on August 21, 1995, and because of the Death Penalty allegation, the *Hovey* Voir Dire was very time-consuming. It wasn't until October 11, 1995, when the actual second trial commenced.

In his Opening Statement, David Conn said that the brothers were motivated by greed when they ambushed their parents. He used the autopsy and crime scene photos to illustrate the brothers had purposely shot their parents in such a way to make it look like a mob hit. In the second trial, the emphasis was on the manner in which they shot their parents. David wanted the jurors to recognize it for what it was, downright ***greed and nothing else***. He explained to the jury how the brothers had carried their dead parents' safe to the home of a probate attorney within 24 hours after they murdered their parents. He showed that the brothers were trying to get their hands on their parents' money as fast as they could in order to spend it.

Next, Erik's attorney, Leslie Abramson, gave her Opening Statement claiming that the brothers killed out of mind-numbing, adrenaline-pumping fear that their parents would kill them for threatening to expose the family secrets. Leslie said, "We will prove to you that Erik was tortured, terrorized, exploited, molested, and abused to such a state he lived in a constant state of fear." It appeared that Leslie 'didn't get the memo' that said that the Defense wasn't going to be able to use the 'Battered Persons Syndrome' Defense. She seemed to be stuck in Auto-Pilot retrying the case the same way she did in the first trial. She was present when the issue was litigated and the Defense had lost, but she was ignoring the fact that the rules had been changed as a result of those losses.

Lyle's Deputy Public Defender, Charles Gessler, apparently 'had gotten the memo' that sexual abuse approach wasn't going to be permitted without evidence. Gessler used his Opening Statement to explain the brothers believed their parents had supernatural powers and knew everything about their sons' activities. The public defender described the prosecution's theory of the brothers wanting their parents' money was wrong, because Lyle and Erik thought that their parents had disowned them. That type of Defense might make sense if there had been no evidence showing the brothers had hired a computer expert to make sure their mother's computer didn't contain a new will.

The following graphic page shows some of the differences in the second trial.

Graphic 12

SECOND MENENDEZ TRIAL

Judge Weisberg changed his ruling about the child abuse unless evidence was presented in court.

Prosecutor David Conn

Author researching legal issues

Lyle Menendez tell all book

Author prepared visual downtown & taken to the Van Nuys court

HOW ERIK MENENDEZ PUT HIS STORY TOGETHER

WHAT CAN THE PROSECUTION PROVE:	WHAT I NEED TO SAY TO GET WHERE I WANT TO GO:	WHERE I WANT TO GO:
Guns purchased two days earlier		Voluntary Manslaughter based on a Self Defense type of Argument
Went on fishing trip unarmed		
Confessed to Oziel & Cignarelli		
ETC.		

Visual used in Argument

ONE APPROACH TO THE EVALUATION OF THE EVIDENCE

COUNT 1- FIRST DEGREE MURDER of Jose Menendez

Is Lyle Menendez Guilty of first degree murder? ☐

If so, is the special circumstance of lying in wait true? ☐

Is Erik Menendez Guilty of first degree murder? ☐

If so, is the special circumstance of lying in wait true? ☐

COUNT 2- FIRST DEGREE MURDER of Mary Louise Menendez

Is Lyle Menendez Guilty of first degree murder? ☐

If so, is the special circumstance of lying in wait true? ☐

Is Erik Menendez Guilty of first degree murder? ☐

If so, is the special circumstance of lying in wait true? ☐

IN REGARD TO COUNTS 1 &2- Multiple Murder Convictions

Is the special circumstance allegation that Lyle Menendez has been convicted of more than one count of murder in this proceeding true? ☐

Is the special circumstance allegation that Erik Menendez has been convicted of more than one count of murder in this proceeding true? ☐

COUNT 3- CONSPIRACY TO COMMIT MURDER

Is Lyle Menendez Guilty of Conspiracy to commit murder? ☐

Is Erik Menendez Guilty of Conspiracy to commit murder? ☐

Author prepared this check list for the jury to follow

CHAPTER 52 PROSECUTION'S CASE

After the three Opening Statements, the jurors had to be totally confused. It didn't seem like all three were on the same page, but things were about to start in a completely new and totally different trial. The prosecution immediately started to set the tone by playing three tapes before the jury. The first tape played was of the brothers, both being interviewed by the detectives at the police station about a month after the shootings. The brothers were asked if they had had any problems with their parents, to which they claimed they didn't. This tape seemed to nail the brothers down solid in that there weren't any claims of abuse. They were in a safe environment-when they were at the police station, a safe place where they could have easily mentioned any type of abuse.

The second tape involved the brothers admitting to Dr. Owens they had killed their parents. This was the tape that had been prohibited from being played without the brothers waiving their privilege. Since the Defense had played it in the first trial, they had clearly waived any privilege they might have had. This tape made the brothers sound like **cold-hearted killers** without a conscious. Undoubtedly, that hit a high note for some of the jurors who were familiar with Paula Abdul's top hit that year, ***Cold Hearted***. They were locked in a scenario where they had the burden of explaining the justification for their actions.

The third and last tape played for the jury was the 9-1-1 tape of the brothers calling the Beverly Hills Police Department dispatcher reporting a crime. What this tape showed was the web of lies, after the killings, in which they turned on the tears so they would not be suspected of being the shooters.

Then it was time for the prosecution to call witnesses. With some of the witnesses, it was déjà vu time. Officer Michael Butkus once again explained that he was the first officer to respond to the 9-1-1 call. He was perplexed when he was walking in front of the house since there was no one around. The dispatcher was talking to the brothers inside and told them to go outside and meet with the responding officers. After a minute or two, the silence was broken by two young men who came running out of the front door screaming something like, "Oh my God, I can't believe it." The officer testified, "My fellow officers and I were shocked, not knowing whether these were suspects, victims, or merely pranksters." This witness gave a snapshot view to the jury of the grisly crime scene.

Then, Detective Les Zoeller was introduced to the jurors. First, he explained his qualifications as a detective by stating he started in law enforcement as an officer in the small city of Gardena in 1971. After several years of working there, he transferred to the Beverly Hills Police Department, where he drove a black-and-white unit around the quiet streets for years. Finally, in 1980, he took the Detective exam, passed, and went on to work in the Detective Bureau. He was only there a short time before he found himself as the lead detective in the Joe Hunt case. As a result of that case, he worked closely with prosecutors, learning how to shore up a publicity case from the ground up.

David Conn used Detective Zoeller to be the eyes of the jurors to view the crime scene. He related to the jury that he and his partner, Tom Linelan, arrived at 1:00 a.m. The brothers were not present but had been transported to the police station. The sergeant. in charge directed him to the family, room where he saw the two dead bodies. As he moved closer to the victims, he could see shotgun pellets sprinkled in the massive craters in each body. Some of the wounds had shotgun wadding in them, meaning the weapon had been fired at extremely close range. At that point, he was certain that the murder weapon was a shotgun. His natural instinct was to start looking for the shell casings, but he didn't find any on the floor or in the cushions of the sofa.

Detective Zoeller maneuvered himself around the coffee table to examine the female victim's body. What he noticed was that her shoes had blood on the bottom of them. This meant the female victim had been standing at some point during the attack. He noticed the female victim's hands had been shot from the outside, as though she had her hands up to cover her eyes and face. This was surprising since most victims hold their palms out toward an attacker. Did this victim recognize the shooters and want to close her eyes to her attacker? It was like the words from the top record of the year, Chicago's ***"Look Away Look Away."*** It can only be imagined, the pain Kitty must have felt seeing her two dear sons blasting away at her, and all of this may have been too painful for her to view.

At that point, Detective Zoeller inspected what Kitty had in her hand. He carefully removed the item from her and found it was Erik's admission papers to UCLA. The irony of the situation was that Kitty had been trying to figure out where Erik had to go to enroll in his freshman classes. It was doubtful the jurors picked up the significance of how hard Kitty had tried to help her children at every step of their lives.

Detectives have to depersonalize a homicide scene. Det. Zoeller noticed on the coffee table a large glass that had a residue of whipped cream and some type of berries. Apparently, these victims were acting as other human beings might on a Sunday evening, sitting on the sofa, enjoying a James Bond video, and eating some berries and cream. The question the jury would have to decide on was, how threatening, at that moment in time, were these parents to their two sons.

Detective Zoeller had to make an executive decision, and that was whether to turn the volume down on the large TV in the family room. None of the officers wanted to disturb the crime scene, so everyone let the TV continue to blare. Zoeller figured for the sanity of all the CSI team there was no need to have the TV looping over and over ***"The Spy Who Loved Me."*** He took it upon himself to turn the video off.

Detective Zoeller left the family room and viewed the rest of the house. He was looking for the shell casings and any weapon that may have been used. After searching every room, the only weapon he found was an unloaded .22 rifle in Kitty's closet, but no shotgun or shell casings were ever found anywhere inside or outside the house. Zoeller remained at the house to oversee the collection of the crime scene evidence. At 4:45 a.m., the coroner's investigators arrived to do their investigation and remove the bodies. Shotgun crime scenes are anything but pretty. While the coroner's staff was picking up Jose's body, they noticed the brain matter had rolled onto the floor. The obvious question for the moment was whether the coroner's investigator should try to replace the brain matter in Jose's head or place it in a separate plastic bag to be placed in the body bag. Only 'special people' are employed by the Coroner's Office, due to the nature of the business. The Coroner's Office is always looking for people to fill vacant positions that they seem to have difficulty filling.

Around 5:30 a.m., the brothers came by asking if they could retrieve their tennis rackets, since they had a match that they had to play. The detectives told them they were still processing the crime scene but they could come back later. At 8:30 a.m., the brothers returned, insisting they needed to obtain their tennis equipment. At that point, the brothers were not considered suspects but mere grieving family. They were told not to go into the family room but they could go upstairs and retrieve their personal belongings.

CHAPTER 53 PEOPLE'S WITNESSES

Perry Bryan, a friend of Lyle's, testified he was trying to get together with the brothers that evening. First they were going to meet for food at the Taste of LA, which didn't work out. Later it was agreed they would meet at the Cheesecake Factory in downtown Beverly Hills. He was disappointed again since they didn't show up as promised. The other topic he testified to was how Jose was disappointed with Lyle's taste in women and was a strict parent with the brothers. He was a witness that didn't add much to the prosecution's case but set the record straight that Jose was certainly trying to work with his sons and hoping something would force them to change their ways.

The next witness was Randy Whitney (pseudonym), the probate attorney who testified that after the shooting the brothers contacted him on how to go about probating their parents' will. Erik mentioned he thought the killings might possibly be a Mafia hit. The following day, the brothers brought to his house a safe. Lyle indicated, while in the presence of Erik, they had opened the safe and found it was empty. Later that day, an uncle discovered a copy of a will from 1981, in which the brothers were named the sole beneficiaries. The brothers mentioned that Jose might have been changed his will and they were checking on the family's computer to see if there was a more recent one.

Howard Edwards (pseudonym) was called next and related how Lyle had contacted him about a computer emergency. He went to the Menendez house on Elm Street and examined the home computer. Lyle was interested in searching for certain files by keywords "will," "Lyle," "Erik" and "Menendez." He was able to find some files, but when he opened them, they were empty. When he advised Lyle the files were empty, he was told to erase the complete hard drive because they were selling the computer and didn't want any family business on it.

Richard Wojdak (pseudonym), a bodyguard, was called next. He had been hired by Lyle to protect him when he was on the East Coast. Lyle told him the Colombian Cartel or Mafia had killed his parents and may be after him. A week later, Lyle told him his services were no longer necessary since his uncle had made a deal with "them."

Next witness to testify was Carlos Brewer (pseudonym), who said two months before the shooting Jose had told him that he wanted to disinherit his sons because they were a big disappointment. The prosecutor asked him if he knew of any sexual abuse being committed by Jose, to which the witness replied he had never heard or seen anything like that. On cross-examination, Leslie asked this witness to explain why Jose wanted to disinherit the boys. He replied there were a number of things but as to Lyle, his father couldn't understand why he wasn't taking advantage of attending an Ivy League school, such as Princeton. When asked about Erik, the witness said Jose was displeased with Erik's lack of toughness, which Jose believed was necessary to be successful.

One of the strange parts of the Menendez's case was how it was so interconnected to the Billionaire Boys Club case. It was well established that the brothers got the idea for the killing of their parents from watching the TV miniseries of the BBC. However, the tentacles of the Joe Hunt's case continued to reach into the heart of the Menendez case. What was uncanny was that Lyle wrote a letter to Adair Eslaminia, (pseudonym) a classmate of Erik's at Beverly Hills High School. If the name "Eslaminia" has a familiar ring to it, you would be correct. The second victim in the BBC case was Hedayat Eslaminia, who was kidnapped by Joe Hunt and company. Hedayat Eslaminia died as they were transporting him in a steamer trunk from Northern California to Los Angeles. It was his son, Tasa Eslaminia, who was involved in setting his dad up in order to raise money for Joe Hunt's Billionaire Boys Club.

What Lyle did was to ask Adair Eslaminia to falsely testify that he and the brothers had asked him to loan them a handgun. The prosecution called Adair as a witness to explain how Lyle was trying to be deceptive, wanting witnesses to lie for him. Lyle's public defender, Gessler, had Adair further admit the plot was never carried out. However, that didn't diminish the fact of the brothers' attempts to be deceptive.

It started with the prosecution not calling Dr. Irwin Gordon, the coroner-medical examiner, who had testified in the first trial. In 1995, Dr. Gordon was not called in the O. J. Simpson case because of mistakes he had made in the autopsy of those victims. David Conn wanted a stronger coroner, one who could be more definite as to how many shots each victim suffered and the sequence of the shots.

The prosecution wanted to put pressure on the defendants as to how the brothers had shot their parents. Robert Lawrence, a private pathologist, was called to the witness stand to testify that both victims had been shot in the legs in order to make the murders appear to be hits by the mafia. There were no shots to the torso of either victim.

Then the DA brought in their star witness, Roger McCarthy, from Failure Analysis Associates, who did a reconstruction of a shot by shot using a computer-generated re-creation of the murders. He testified that the brothers surprised their parents as they sat in front of the TV. It showed the brothers purposely shot at their parents' kneecaps to make the killings look like a Mafia hit.

Showing that the victims were both seated was contrary to what the brothers had claimed, which was their parents were initially standing when they were shot. On cross-examination, Lyle's attorney, Gessler, attacked McCarthy's qualifications and questioned why he had not contacted the coroner or criminalists who were at the crime scene. The Defense went to great lengths to cast doubts on McCarthy's reconstructions, implying there were too many variables that couldn't be factored in. The prosecution's purpose for this witness was to show that the shooting was premeditated, from start to finish, and not a 'blind panic' the brothers had claimed in the first trial.

By David Conn placing the emphasis on the method and manner in the killings of the victims, the entire second jury trial took on a different dimension. The focus of the case was no longer directed at the brothers being abused but now was on the debate as to the manner in which the brothers had maliciously killed their parents. The bottom line for the prosecution was, it really didn't matter whether the brothers were intentionally trying to shoot the kneecaps of their folks or not. As long as the Defense continued to fight that issue, the jurors were continuing to have to visualize how heinous it was for any child to shoot their parents with a shotgun. By November 20, 1995, Prosecutor Conn rested the People's case after calling only 30 witnesses.

CHAPTER 54 DEFENSE EVIDENCE

The Defense needed a wakeup call to realize this wasn't going to be a repeat of the first trial. The Defense's first witness called was Martin Fackler, an expert on wound ballistics who testified that the prosecution's reconstruction by Roger McCarthy could not be considered scientific because it contained too many errors and too many variables. This Defense witness spent time attacking the reconstruction, claiming certain facts were left out. However, on cross-examination, when David Conn asked which specific facts were wrong, the witness couldn't answer. With further questioning, it was clear the Defense's expert wasn't familiar with the facts of the crime scene as much so as the prosecution's witness, McCarthy.

Erik's attorney, Leslie Abramson, called Ron Linhart, the Assistant Director of the Los Angeles County Sheriff's Department Crime Lab, who testified the blood spatter analysis contradicted much of McCarthy's reconstruction model. Linhart believed the parents had to have been standing at some point during the shooting. Then, Dwight Van Horn testified that McCarthy's reconstruction was nothing more than 'junk science.' Van Horn had been used in the first trial by the prosecution. The Prosecutor, David Conn, then asked a very sensitive question that brought everything in focus. David asked if the Sheriff's Department thought their Crime Lab should have been consulted by the DA's Office, instead of going to an outside source such as Roger McCarthy. David was able to show to the jury that there was a 'mini-turf war' going on between the Sheriff's Department and the DA's Office.

The Defense then called a nationally well-known expert, Dr. Cyril Wecht, a pathologist from Pennsylvania. When he took the witness stand, he quickly declared McCarthy's reconstruction of the shootings was doomed to failure since all the witnesses were moving about. This pointed up one of the difficulties with a reconstruction model, in that it is isolated to a precise time. In a dynamic crime scene, both the victims and shooters are constantly moving about.

A forensic expert, Charles Morton, testified to blood spatters and shotgun pellet holes. He said that the physical evidence showed Kitty was standing when she was shot. Jose's clothes indicated he was standing as well. By this time, the jurors may have been wondering why the Defense was calling all these witnesses to disprove Roger McCarthy's reconstruction. It didn't make any difference as to the guilt or innocence of the brothers whether their parents were standing up or sitting down, when they were mowed down by the multiple shots from the shotguns. **David Conn's trial tactic was brilliant, in that the jurors' attention was focused on the brutality of the brothers and not whether they had suffered some form of child abuse at the hands of their father.**

Now it was 'ShowTime' for the defendants to take the witness stand to tell their story. As to the two brothers testifying, everyone would agree that Lyle did the best job of testifying in the first trial. Erik was not as captivating and was easily confused when he was cross-examined by the prosecutors. Because of Lyle's giant mistake of telling a reporter he had snowed the first jury, it was no longer viable to have Lyle testify for the Defense. If he had testified, the DA would have asked him what he meant when he said, "***I can move a jury, I think. I get very emotional...I just affect people more.***" If the second jury heard those statements, Lyle's credibility would be less than zero.

Could Erik rise to the occasion and tell a convincing story? On December 6, 1995, Erik took the witness stand and swore to tell the truth. For 15 days, Erik did his best to testify and be convincing. He claimed his parents had been violent in dealing with him and his brother. He described how his father beat and molested him from a very young age all the way to the present. He also included his mother in committing the abuse by the mere fact she humiliated and degraded him. He continued to testify that he loved his parents and he didn't kill them out of hatred but because he and his brother feared they would kill them first since they thought they would reveal the alleged sexual abuse. Erik testified that Jose told him he and Lyle had been written out of the their will because they weren't living up to his expectations

After eight days of trying to keep everything straight, it was time for the cross-examination from the prosecutor. David Conn started reviewing all the times Erik had lied to the police, his family, and friends during the first six months after the shooting. Conn raised a few logical questions with Erik. If he was truly being molested when he was 18 years old, why didn't he move out since he had money and a car? Conn took it one step further and asked, why didn't he join the Army to get away from the molestation? Erik's response was the Army couldn't protect him from this father, the most powerful man he ever knew. When the prosecutor asked him who could verify any act involving sexual abuse, Erik replied that no living person could corroborate his or his brother's sexual abuse.

Since Erik had tendered his mental state as part of this Defense, he had to undergo a psychological exam by the prosecution's expert, Dr. Dietz. Erik ended his testimony by claiming he and his brother did not concoct the stories of child abuse in order to avoid a murder conviction. John Wilson, a psychology professor from Cleveland State University, testified that Erik suffered from Post-Traumatic Stress Disorder at the time he killed his parents. This disorder caused nightmares and amnesia. What caused Erik's disorder were the repeated acts of sexual, physical, and psychological abuse. This was the only Defense expert witness the jury would hear from in the second trial.

On January 12, 1996, Charles Gessler started Lyle's defense completely different than expected. The public had been waiting all these weeks thinking that Lyle would again take the witness stand and disclose all the derogatory allegations against his father. Most people didn't realize that he had 'cooked his goose' when he told a reporter how he had deceived the first jury. Now his new attorney was trying to create a new Defense, which was that the killings were done in the 'heat of passion' when his fear and anger overwhelmed him. Since Lyle didn't testify, his attorney wasn't able to use Lyle's testimony to show what the source of the 'heat of passion' was that had consumed him. Also, he didn't testify to any child abuse and he was precluded from calling any child abuse experts to testify about his state of mind.

Originally in the first trial the brothers had a joint defense claiming that they were victims of 'Battered Person Syndrome.' But in this second trial, Lyle's attorney, Gessler, called very few witnesses and it was not clear to the jurors what Lyle's Defense really was.

Even Dr. William Vega, who was Erik's psychiatrist when he was in custody, was not called as a witness. His testimony was held to be irrelevant to the issues raised in the second trial.

CHAPTER 55 PROSECUTORS' REBUTTAL

The prosecution was faced with a myriad of things to respond to. They started by calling Craig Curry, who had been Erik's closest friend when they were living in Calabasas. They were both promising tennis players. He testified that shortly after the shooting, Erik invited him over to the house on Elm Street. Erik related to him exactly how he and his brother had killed their folks. He started by explaining where his brother's Alfa Romeo had been parked and that it contained the two shotguns in the trunk. He told him how they snuck into the family room without being seen by their sleeping parents. When Erik got to the family room, he pointed out where his folks had been sitting and where he was standing when he shot his mom.

Craig related to the jury he had to do some soul searching as to what he should do. He and Erik had spent so much time together and he thought of Erik as part of his family when he lived in Calabasas. Craig was experiencing a tug-of-war. Should he go to the police and report what Erik had told him? Obviously Erik, without a doubt, trusted him, and he didn't want to betray his trust. Craig said it took him three months to make a decision to contact the police and explain what Erik had told him in confidence. It made him feel bad he had betrayed Erik's trust, and he didn't want to hurt his friend. So, he told the complete story, then added that he later denied it.

Next, David Conn, the prosecutor, wanted to show the jury the tale that Erik tried to weave before them in regards to the toupee incident had been all made up. To poke a hole through the story, Jaime Pincus, the former girlfriend of Lyle's was called to testify. She testified that Erik knew Lyle wore a hairpiece as early as 1988. Therefore, he was lying when he claimed he didn't know anything about the toupee until, allegedly, Kitty grabbed it off Lyle's head shortly before the shooting.

Conn then called Dr. Dietz, who had an opportunity to interview Erik, as a witness to rebut the claim Erik suffered from a 'Post-Traumatic Stress Disorder.' Dr. Dietz testified it was impossible to diagnosis Erik with this disorder because there was no way of knowing if the so-called child abuse had actually occurred or not. He also didn't suffer from a 'learned helplessness' syndrome either, since he and his brother had bought two shotguns, he had loaded the one, and went to the shooting range to learn how to fire the weapon. These actions are inconsistent with the passiveness of 'learned helplessness.'

At that point, the final witness had testified and the evidentiary phase of the trial was over. The jurors were most likely the ones who were most relieved when both the DA and the Defense said they "Rest." It was now the judge's job to decide on what Jury Instructions to give.

The judge ruled that there was insufficient evidence the brothers were in 'imminent danger' when they fatally shot their parents, so their request for instruction on the so-called "imperfect self-defense" was ruled out. At the end of the first trial, this was the law the Defense so effectively had argued to the jury. The judge agreed with the Defense that they could argue that the brothers shot Jose in the 'heat of passion.' What that gave the Defense was a way of avoiding a Murder conviction and receiving a lesser conviction for Voluntary Manslaughter. The judge found there was no evidence to show that Kitty had provoked her sons, so the Defense of 'heat of passion' would NOT apply to the killing of Kitty.

The Defense could see the law spelled out in the Jury Instructions was not as beneficial this time as it had been in the first trial. Both Erik's and Lyle's attorneys had to structure their Arguments to fit the new rules the judge had laid out.

On February 20, 1996, Prosecutor David Conn rose from the counsel table and walked over to the lectern to begin his Argument. David made eye contact with every juror by slowly scanning all 12 jurors. Then he addressed the jurors as a group and started his meticulous summation of the case. Peering through his glasses, he was a spitting image of Clark Kent, as though he was addressing the editorial board of the Daily Planet newspaper. David had the attention of the jurors, but he knew he had so much to cover and that his challenge would be how to keep their attention. He knew he had to get it right and answer every question any of the jurors might have. He couldn't afford even one juror getting lost and hanging up the jury.

This was a strange type of case to argue for the prosecution in that the defendants admitted to doing the killings and clearly did it with the intent to kill. So the prosecutor didn't need to spend any time linking the defendants to the crime. The only thing the prosecutor needed to do was knock down whatever the Defense was going to claim and how it didn't apply. David scoffed at the brothers' claim of abuse as "the silliest, most ridiculous story ever told in a courtroom." The jurors had heard the story so many times of 'Kitty grabbing Lyle's toupee' and Erik being shocked to the core, the jurors started to smile whenever it was reiterated by some witness or one of the attorneys. The prosecutor only had to mention Jaime Pincus's revelation about how Erik had known about the toupee for years. As the brothers sat there at the counsel table, they must have mused to themselves, if only they had thought up a more credible story than the 'flying toupee.'

David's attack on the Defense was done by turning over and looking under every stone. He showed them that there was nothing there. He also demonstrated his personal disdain by injecting sarcasm and, to some extent, belittling the Defense. After his thorough examination, there weren't any questions that went unanswered. He reviewed with the jury Erik's testimony, which was self-serving and filled with lies, as he pointed out endless inconsistencies. David encouraged the jury to reject Erik's claim that his father sexually abused him, since there was no corroboration by any person or physical evidence to support his allegation.

The prosecution's Argument seriously undermined any of the possible Defenses. So when it was time for Erik's attorney, Leslie Abramson, to argue, she came out swinging. She went into a tirade of accusing the prosecutor of presenting fraudulent witnesses in an effort to win a case for political reasons. Her logic was that the Los Angeles County District Attorney was under pressure to try to win a "big case" since they had lost the McMartin preschool molestation cases, the first Menendez trial, and the O. J. Simpson murder trial. There appeared to be some type of disconnect, because she ranted and raved about the prosecutor, which had nothing to do with the validity of her Defense.

Then she attacked the prosecution for playing the tape of her client confessing to the crime. This didn't make sense since she and her client had waived their privilege by using the tape in the first trial. She objected to the prosecution's claim the brothers had shot their parents in the knees to make it look like a mob hit. What was outlandish about her Argument was the fact that it was the brothers who had told the police, immediately after the shooting, that it could be a 'mob hit.'

Leslie Abramson also argued that her client had Post-Traumatic Stress Disorder and Erik was in a state of mind at the time of the killings where he did not harbor malice. She was desperately trying to sell the fact that Erik had some type of disorder, but it wasn't clear what that had to do with his killing his parents. Finally, Leslie's Argument took on a personal plea, in that she had become so close to Erik that if the jury convicted him it would be the ultimate tragedy in her life. Some of the jurors must have wondered what her personal plea had to do with proving whether or not Erik was guilty of murdering his parents.

After three days, Leslie finished her Argument and it was time for Lyle's attorney, Gessler, to argue his case. His approach was 180 degrees from Leslie's. Gessler walks and talks like a law professor. He knows the law inside out and has a vast experience in homicide trials because of his long and distinctive career with the Public Defender's Office. His first attack was on the prosecution's theory of the case that the brothers killed their parents for the money. He argued that Lyle knew he and Erik had been disinherited from their parents' estate. Then he asked, why would the brothers kill their parents, who were the only source of support they had? If they killed their parents, they would lose everything. He emphasized the brothers were the last persons who would want any harm to come to their parents.

What Gessler said made perfect sense, if the issue was whether they killed their parents. However, the brothers admitted to the shooting, so Gessler's argument didn't fit the facts. Then he took another approach: he asked the jury to find Lyle guilty of only Manslaughter and not guilty of any crime for his mother. The logic of such an argument seemed to escape everyone: on what ground do you ignore the fact that Lyle said he shot at his mother?

Gessler realized he had been placed in a checkmate situation, but he tried his best to find a way to save his client. He argued that Jose caused his own death by molesting his sons and causing them to believe they could not escape his grasp. Since Lyle didn't testify, there was NO direct evidence of Lyle being molested by Jose.

Gessler had to discuss Kitty's involvement. He tried to make it seem like it was Kitty's fault. He argued that Kitty brought about her own death by not protecting her sons and by making the brothers believe she was an enforcer of her husband's abuse. As strange as this Argument seemed, one had to wonder if Lyle's attorney was saying under his breath, "Lyle, why did you have to tell the writer what a great job you did in deceiving the first jury?" Lyle's cockiness had placed his attorney in a 'straightjacket' that no one could fight their way out of.

The prosecution was permitted to give a short Rebuttal Argument. Dave Conn pointed out how both of the brothers' attorneys had spent most of their Argument blaming their parents. They had to weave a web of lies to justify their heinous crime of Murder in the first degree of both Jose and Kitty Menendez.

On March 1, 1966, the jury started their deliberations. The deliberations went on for two weeks without a verdict. This didn't look good for the DA's Office, especially since this trial had been more condensed and with fewer witnesses. The trial was also taking a toll on the physical health of the jurors. The foreperson had a heart attack and a woman had premature labor. Those jurors had to be replaced and the entire deliberation had to start over.

Six days later after this newly composed jury started their deliberation, a verdict was arrived at. They concluded both brothers were guilty of two first degree

Murders, plus the Conspiracy to commit Murder charge. Also, the special circumstances of 'Lying in wait' and 'Multiple Murder' were found to be true; therefore, the case would have to go on to the Penalty Phase.

CHAPTER 56 PENALTY PHASE

To one knew more about the law pertaining to the Death Penalty than David Conn. He had published a notebook on all the Death Penalty appellate opinions, which had become the bible for all prosecutors, as well as most judges. So, when David spoke on Death Penalty issues he had all the case law to back him up. On March 22, 1996, the judge had brought the jurors back and they were advised the penalty phase of the trial would begin. He explained the legal procedure was different in that they would be presented with aggravating or mitigating evidence. They would have to decide if the Aggravating Factors substantially outweighed the Mitigating Factors. If they found the Aggravating Factors DID outweigh the Mitigating Factors, then the penalty would be DEATH. If not, then the penalty would be LIFE WITHOUT THE POSSIBILITY OF PAROLE, better known by attorneys as 'LWOP.'

The DA started off by presenting more evidence, showing the brutal manner in which the brothers had killed their parents. Witnesses were called to show the callousness of the killing. The Defense wanted to show all the Mitigating evidence such as that the brothers were young and naïve and could live productive lives in prison.

On April 4, 1996, Leslie Abramson called Dr. Vega, who had testified he had seen Erik as a patient and treated him for several years while he was in the County jail. In his professional opinion, Erik had emotional issues he tried to treat him for. David Conn asked to see the psychiatrist's notes and reports. Dr. Vega handed over his reports. The prosecutor asked if that was all the reports. At that point, the temperature in the courtroom went past the boiling point. It became so quiet that you could almost hear attorney Leslie Abramson's heart beating louder and faster than humanly possible.

David Conn, the prosecutor, was standing at counsel table when he removed from a manila envelope some 14 pages of a report. David asked the court, "May I approach this witness?" He walked up to the witness stand. Dr. Vega's eyes were fixed on the report in the prosecutor's hand. As he stepped within three feet of the witness, the prosecutor said, "Have you seen this psychiatric report of Erik Menendez?" The witness, in a whisper said, "The Defense Attorney told me to delete parts of the report, so I took out 14 pages." Pandemonium erupted in the courtroom. THE DEFENSE HAD BEEN CAUGHT WITHHOLDING EVIDENCE FROM THE DA.

The judge recessed the trial until the next day in order to hold a hearing, out of the presence of the jury. Leslie Abramson was called as a witnesses and she immediately took the Fifth Amendment and refused to answer any questions since it might incriminate her. She refused to answer two questions about her possible misconduct. Then Erik's co-counsel, Barry Levine, made a motion for a mistrial on the basis that Erik's lead attorney, Leslie Abramsons, had ineffectively represented him.

For a prosecutor, it seemed odd that Erik was demanding a mistrial because of something his attorney had done on his behalf. It was hard to know if that was circular logic or not. However, the judge ruled Barry Levine was perfectly capable to take over Erik's case for the penalty phase and the mistrial motion was denied and thrown in the legal trash bin.

On April 6, David Conn told the court how he learned about the deleted notes. Originally, Abramson had given Conn, under a continuing discovery order, Vega's notes, which had parts deleted. Months later, there was a hearing in the Van Nuys courthouse in which Conn needed to review Vega's notes. However, he realized his copy had been left in his Downtown office. Conn asked Dr. Dietz if he had a copy, which he didn't. But Dr. Dietz said he would ask Dr. Vega for a copy, since he had a good rapport with him. As a result, Dr. Vega gave Dr. Dietz an extra copy of the original report from the Defense. Later Conn compared the extra copy with the Discovery version and found the Discovery version was missing 14 pages and Dr. Vega had reworked 10 pages of his notes.

The deleted notes contained some very incriminating statements from Erik. It talked about what it would be like to live without his parents. Erik and Lyle were planning something drastic. Erik told Dr. Vega a story about how his father's homosexual lover visited the mansion two days before the murders. Later Dr. Vega asked Erik about those statements and he told him that the story was a lie.

April 9, 1996, out of the presence of the jury, Defense attorneys Gessler and Levine sought to have Abramson removed from the case because her continued presence in the case would be detrimental for both defendants. This entire situation was weighing heavily on Erik. He asked the judge if he could talk to him alone in chambers. The judge agreed to permit him to address him alone in chambers. The end result was that Judge Weisberg allowed Leslie Abramson to remain as counsel but she had to remain mute. The judge ordered the prosecutors not to mention in front of the jury anything about Abramson's order to delete his notes. The DA could impeach Dr. Vega's testimony without making any references to Abramson.

On April 10, Dr. Vega's questioning as a Defense witness was finished and the DA put on three more witnesses. On April 11, David Conn argued that the brothers should be sentenced to death because they chose to kill their parents in a horrifying and brutal manner.

During Conn's Argument, he ridiculed the Defense for allegations of psychological abuse, saying the Defense was desperate and trivial. Barry Levine accused the prosecution of arbitrarily deciding who was eligible for the Death Penalty. He claimed that the prosecution had not shown any Aggravation besides the crime itself. On April 12, the jury started their deliberations. After several days, on April 17, the jury came back with a sentence of Life Without Possibility of Parole on both brothers.

After the trial, some of the jurors said that they gave great weight to the fact that the brothers had no criminal record of violence. A few jurors were sympathetic to the brothers and believed their upbringing maybe was at fault. Some didn't believe they did it for the money, but for the thrill of getting away with it.

On July 2, 1996, Judge Weisberg sentenced them to LWOP on both murder charges and conspiracy to commit murder, thus ending a six-year journey through the mysterious criminal justice system. Also on the same day, the two brothers did a TV interview with Barbara Walters for the TV program 20/20. The question was why they would kill their parents, who had done so much for them? They acted like celebrities and maintained they were the true victims of the trial. The purpose of the interview was for them to make an appeal to the media that they wanted to serve their time together at the same state prison facility.

After initial processing, the California Department of Corrections decided to separate the two brothers; therefore, they ended up serving their sentences at separate state prison facilities.

CHAPTER 57 EERIE SIMILARITIES TO LOEB AND LEOPOLD CASE

The Loeb and Leopold case gripped the imagination of the entire country during the mid-1920s. Loeb was from a wealthy family in Chicago. He was incredibly brilliant and spoke 27 languages fluently. He graduated as the youngest person from the University of Michigan. His intellectual curiosity led him to study Fredrick Nietzsche's theory of the Superhuman race. That philosophy claimed that certain people are above the law because of their intellect.

Loeb was attending the University of Chicago, School of Law, where he met a fellow student, Nathan Leopold, who had grown up in the wealthy district of Chicago. His father was a lawyer and later became a vice president of Sears Roebuck and Company. Loeb and Leopold became the best of friends and wanted to prove to others they were so smart that they definitely could commit the Perfect Crime and get away with it. They started out committing petty theft and even some vandalism to illustrate they couldn't be caught. However, they were disappointed that their crimes didn't receive any media attention. That was when they decided to commit a more serious crime that would generate media publicity.

After weeks of preparation, the two friends were ready to commit a murder. On Wednesday, January 21, 1924, they rented a car and started driving around the

Kenwood area of Chicago. Richard Loeb had attended the ***Harvard School for Boys,*** where the rich kids of Chicago attended. (Strange, it was almost the same name as the ***Harvard Prep School*** the boys from the Billionaire Boys Club case had attended). They agreed to find a rich kid and kidnap him. While canvassing the area they saw Bobby Franks, who was 14 years old, waiting for a ride. Loeb recognized him since he was a second cousin of his and he had played tennis at the Loeb family tennis court.

The boys pulled up alongside and asked him if he wanted a ride, to which he said "No." Loeb thought fast as to a reason why they needed to talk. He mentioned he wanted to talk to him about a special tennis racket that Bobby Franks had. With that comment, Bobby got in the front passenger seat and they drove off. A short distance away, Loeb, who was in the backseat, took out a chisel and hit the victim over the head several times. As Leopold drove, Loeb pulled the victim into the backseat and killed him.

Loeb and Leopold were pleased the killing went as planned. They covered the body with a blanket and went to an eating establishment and had dinner. After it turned dark, they drove to an isolated area near a railroad culvert, where they dragged the body out of the car. They didn't want the body identified, so they removed the clothing and poured hydrochloric acid all over the body. In the process, Leopold accidently dropped his glasses.

In order to make it look like a kidnap for ransom, Leopold called the victim's mother demanding money. They also typed a ransom note and mailed it to Bobby Franks' family. The family paid the money, expecting the return of little Bobby Franks; however, there was no release of the victim. The crime went unsolved for months. The wealthy people of Chicago were frightened and the pressure on the police was mounting.

A short time later, the body of a young boy was discovered and later determined to be that of Bobby Franks. The detectives were disappointed that there was no significant evidence found at the crime scene. The only thing recovered was a pair of glasses found on the ground near the victim's body. The prescription could fit thousands of people in the Chicago area. However, what was unique about the glasses were the **hinges**. They were a specialty item, and when the police checked with optometrists it was discovered there were only three such pairs of glasses sold in the area. The detectives had all three people come to the police station to be interviewed.

One of them was Nathan Leopold. He said he had lost his glasses and that they must have fallen out of his pocket. The detectives asked him to show them how they could have fallen out of his shirt pocket. He tried to demonstrate how they fell out of his pocket, but the problem was he couldn't replicate how that happened. The detectives became suspicious, but they didn't have any solid evidence against him. Then the detective asked if he had an alibi as to the time of the kidnapping. He said that he was with his good friend Richard Loeb and they were driving around together in his family's car and that they had picked up two girls to take them downtown.

The detectives were getting nowhere fast but needed to keep Leopold at the station for several more hours. Leopold's parents had the family chauffeur drive to the police station with some clean clothes for him. The chauffeur brought the clothes in and gave them to one of the detectives. As the chauffeur was walking out, the detective casually asked a question about the use of the family car on the day of the kidnapping. The chauffeur stated the family car had been at the mechanic's shop and was being worked on.

The detectives had the chauffeur double-check his records and there was no way Leopold could have used the family car. The detectives confronted Leopold with the lie, and he quietly admitted he was involved but it was his good friend, Loeb, who did the killing. When the detectives called in Loeb, he was told Leopold had confessed and said that he was the killer. Loeb reflected on his options and said he was involved but he was not the killer because the killing was done by his partner Leopold.

So both great friends were pointing the finger at the other. When it came time for the trial, the boy's parents retained the top attorney in the country, Clarence Darrow, to represent both boys. When the great orator, Clarence Darrow, saw the facts were stacked up against the boys, he decided to have them plead guilty, in hopes of persuading the judge not to give them the Death Penalty. Darrow commenced a 12-hour argument before the judge explaining why these two boys needed mercy for the heinous crime they committed. He blamed the crime on World War I and the aftermath it created. He argued that no one knew how the killing of thousands during the war had desensitized the public and affected society overall. Many felt it was the finest Argument against the Death Penalty ever presented in a courtroom.

Apparently it had an effect on the judge, who handed down a life sentence for both boys for the murder and 99 years for the kidnapping. Loeb served his time until January 28, 1936, when he was attacked and cut up with a straight-edge razor by his cellmate and died in the prison hospital. However, Leopold was luckier and served 33 years in prison and was released. He moved to Puerto Rico, where he had a productive life working as an X-ray technician in the local hospital. He wrote about his life and finally died on August 29, 1971, at the age of 66.

What were the similarities in all these murders? All these cases involved **RICH KIDS** who thought because of their brilliance they could commit murder and get away with it. Even with their brilliant planning, they somehow slipped up and got caught. In Loeb and Leopold, it was accidently dropping eye glasses that had a unique hinge. With Joe Hunt, he forgot and left his "To Do" list at the crime scene. Finally, the Menendez brothers seemed to get it right except for talking to a psychiatrist who had a resentful ex-girlfriend. (We will further review the mistakes that caught even the smartest killers.)

All these killers were bright and believed their intelligence would allow them to commit the PERFECT MURDER, and never get caught.

CHAPTER 58 COMMITTING THE PERFECT CRIME

What Went Wrong for Joe Hunt and the Billionaire Boys Club?

Using a To Do List-

Leaving a To Do List at victim's house-

Leave a thumb print on the back of the To Do List-

Using his handwriting to write To Do List-

Tell fellow members that he was involved in killing

What Went Wrong for the Menendez Brothers?

Spending Spree-

Erik talking to Psychiatrist-

Lyle threatening Psychiatrist-

Dr. Owens telling girlfriend-

Dr. Owens asking girlfriend to listen in-

Dr. Owens telling girlfriend he had tapes-

Dr. Owens breaking up with girlfriend-

Girlfriend going to police-

Police got search warrant for tapes-

Police asking where are the tapes

Dr. Owens takes them to bank-

Supreme Court ruled that first tape could come in-

Brothers come up with toupee story-

Brothers claim they were molested-

Brothers threaten to tell about molestation-

Brothers claim parents are going to kill them-

Lyle told writer that he deceived first jury-

What Went Wrong for Loeb and Leopold?

Dropping eyeglasses

Having exclusive eye glass frames

Claim driving around with family car

Detective asking chauffeur about the family car

Boys couldn't have used car since it was in the shop

Boy's admission of being involved

Both blamed other for actual killing

CHAPTER 59 WHAT HAVE WE LEARNED ABOUT RICH KIDS COMMITTING MURDER?

If we were asked who are the most likely suspects in a murder investigation, we would most likely describe poor young males from the inner city. Seldom do we think of the rich as being involved in murder. Why is this? You look at wealthy communities like Beverly Hills, a city that can go an entire year without a single homicide. But the adjacent City of Los Angeles will have hundreds of murders every year.

If there are so few rich people involved in killings, then why would these Rich Kids in the cases we just reviewed feel a need to commit murder? Or another way of saying it is, why do young privileged, well-educated young men kill? The initial reaction is that these Rich Kids feel an **entitlement**. But, the few Rich Kids who do commit murder seem to be like Loeb and Leopold. Those two had actually read and believed in the teachings of Fredrick Nietzsche's theory of a Superhuman race. They saw themselves as being different and not bound by the mundane rules and laws that pertain to the masses.

Joe Hunt was handsome and incredibly brilliant. He thought of himself as someone above the madding crowd. He recognized he was the type of person, in society, who thinks outside the box. He didn't have any problem justifying Ron Levin's death. He thought of Levin as a lesser person. The killing of Levin was the mere end to justifying the means. For Joe, it wasn't a matter of weighing on one's conscience, it was a matter of necessity. The idea was to do the killing as methodically as possible so it would not harm but only benefit his Billionaires Boys Club.

There are those who would assign the term **narcissistic** to these Rich Kid killers. Certainly, Joe Hunt seems to fit the definition of a narcissistic personality. By definition, this type of person possesses an exaggerated sense of importance concerning themselves and their works and possesses little or no empathy for others around him. They believe they are superior, special, or unique and expect others to recognize that quality. A person with a narcissistic personality has a distorted sense of entitlement. There was no doubt Joe Hunt lacked empathy for others, especially Ron Levine.

As to the Menendez brothers, they felt a strong **entitlement,** in that they were owed a good life. To them it seemed as if their parents were wrong in trying to cut them out of their will. They felt they were entitled, since their father was trying to force them to go to Ivy League schools, which they didn't want to do. The lack of conscience was exhibited by them when they gunned down their parents. But when you look at all that had been given to them, it only seemed natural they would fight for what they had been conditioned to believe they were entitled to.

A hot topic in psychiatric and legal circles has been the new Defense of **Affluenza**. This new excuse is used to explain why a Rich Kid may not be at fault for committing a crime. The most noted was the Ethan Couch case, which involved a Rich Kid in Texas who killed four innocent victims while driving under the influence of alcohol. The Defense claimed that it wasn't the fault of the rich kid since he was the product of wealthy, privileged parents who never set limits for their son.

All because of his or her upbringing, the Rich Kid never learned that actions have consequences. The claim is that knowing the law isn't sufficient, but what is truly important is that a person must have experienced harmful consequences for his socially inappropriate or illegal behavior in the past. The threat of legal consequence will appear empty if that person hadn't experienced consequences before.

This new concept blames the easy life, or the protected life that insulates Rich Kids from realizing there are consequences when they kill someone. There might be some truth to the fact that Rich Kids are definitely different from the rest of us. This book has tried to provide you, the reader, with insight into the reasons and motives of certain young men who make up the **Rich Kid Killers of Beverly Hills.**

CHAPTER 60 EPILOGUE

JOE HUNT

After the trial involving Ron Levin's death, he and the others went to trial in San Mateo County for the kidnapping and death of Hedayat Eslaminia. Joe took the witness stand, and with his charisma and persuasiveness he was able to convince several jurors that he was not guilty of the charges. The case resulted in a hung jury. The San Mateo DA's Office decided not to retry Joe for Hedayat's death.

On April 10, 1993, he married Tammy Gandolfo on a patio nestled inside a compound of barbed wire, at Folsom state prison. Tammy had worked as a paralegal during his trial in San Mateo. She continued to work as a volunteer on his appeals in the Ron Levin case. Eventually he proposed to her and she couldn't say 'no.'

As of 2014, he was imprisoned at Pleasant Valley, Coalinga, CA

TASA ESLAMINIA (pseudonym)

He went on trial for the kidnap and death of his father in San Mateo and was convicted. Later in 1998, his conviction was reversed by a federal court and the San Mateo DA couldn't locate Dean Kelly, so Tasa was not retried for the killing of his father and was released from Folsom State Prison. On August 11, 2012, he was driving a taxi for Luxor Cab Company in San Francisco when he ran a red light and hit and killed a pedestrian. It seemed weird he started out as one of the richest kids and ended up driving a taxi cab in the city by the Bay.

FRED WAPNER

He stayed on as a prosecutor in the DA's Office until 1989, when he became a judge. He continues to hear felony cases in the Criminal Courts Building in Downtown Los Angeles.

In 2014, his father, Judge Joseph Wapner, celebrated his 94th birthday and is still doing reunions of his famous TV program, ***People's Court.***

LYLE MENENDEZ

On the day before being sentenced he married Playboy Playmate Anna Eriksson, before being shipped off to state prison. Judge Nancy Brown had ordered the brothers be removed from County jail and brought to her courtroom for the ceremony. However, the presiding judge heard about it and cancelled the removal order. Since the brothers didn't get to Judge Brown's courtroom, the judge still conducted the wedding ceremony by phone. Leslie Abramson slipped the ring on the bride's finger, since Lyle was still at the jail. This became a hotly contested issue between various factions of the Superior Court judges. Some were against conducting such a wedding for such a brutal killer. However, with all the commotion, the marriage lasted less than a year when the bride found out Lyle was corresponding with another woman.

With one unsuccessful marriage, Lyle waited until November 21, 2003, to marry Rebecca Sneed, who was a magazine editor; the ceremony took place at the prison.

Lyle has been moved around to various prisons and in 2014 was imprisoned at Mule Creek, near Sacramento, CA.

ERIK MENENDEZ

In 1998, Erik was married to Tammi Saccoman in the Folsom State Prison. They have remained married for a couple years. She later wrote a book titled, "They Said We'd Never Make It." In 2010 a TV documentary known as 'Mrs. Menendez' was made regarding their marriage which addressed the common questions as to why marry a prisoner serving Life.

The prison staff caught him transporting "kites" (This is how prisoners send messages among themselves) for gang members and he was transferred to Pelican Bay Maximum Prison in Crescent City. Later in 2014, he was relocated to RJ Donovan Prison, near San Diego, CA.

DAVID CONN

He was a prosecutor for 18 years. After the Menendez case, he was interviewed by the LA Times newspaper and stated, "I wouldn't mind one day being the Los Angeles District Attorney." Shortly thereafter, he was notified he would be transferred to the Norwalk Branch office. He was passed over for promotion and removed as the deputy in charge of the Special Trials Unit. In 1997, he left the DA's Office and became a private defense attorney with a Century City law firm. In 2006, he died at the age of 56 at his Dana Point home, five months after being diagnosed with amyotrophic lateral sclerosis, known as Lou Gehrig's disease. This was a shock to all who knew and worked with David. He was one of those giants in the legal field, and is sorely missed.

LESLIE ABRAMSON

Because of her actions in telling Dr. Vega to delete notes, there were several investigations. In 1997, after an eleven-month investigation, the DA's Office didn't bring any criminal charges against her for her conduct during the Menendez case. In 1999, the State Bar of California closed their investigation on her, deciding there was insufficient evidence to conclude she violated ethical rules during the Menendez case. She reappeared as a defense attorney in the Phil Spector case for a short period of time, but they parted ways long before the case went to trial. However, she appears to have taken her shingle off the wall and faded into the woodwork, to the pleasure of most judges and prosecutors.

DR. OWENS (pseudonym)

In 1997, he surrendered his psychotherapist license and moved to another state.

The following graphic page provides some internet information about the Menendez brothers.

Graphics 13

EPILOGUE

Lyle married to Anna Eriksson

Erik married Tammi Saccoman

Lyle married to Rebecca Sneed

Author in front of Menendez house today

OTHER BOOKS

By Ronald E Bowers

If you enjoyed this book, take a look at my other books I have written.

My tenth book was titled the *Celebrity Curse.* This book reviewed the mysterious deaths of celebrities starting with the investigation into **Marilyn Monroe's** death. For over a half a century there has been a growing controversy over her untimely death. Was it an accidental overdose or a suicide? However, over the years more facts have revealed the possibility that she may have been murdered. This book considers all the possibilities trying to separate fact from fiction.

Also included in this book is a behind the scenes look at the case of the enablers in the strange death of **Anna Nicole Smith** which resulted in one of the strangest prosecutions of all times. Further on in the ***Celebrity Curse*** we discuss the mysterious deaths of **John Belushi, Natalie Wood** as well as old-time screen legend **Thelma Todd**. Of course the book wouldn't be complete without including the prosecution of **Michael Jackson's** doctor who was giving the superstar an IV drip of Propofol to assist him in sleeping.

Another aspect of the book ***Celebrity Curse*** is a review of a number to Stalking the Stars cases which include **Madonna, Mel Gibson, Catherine Zeta Jones, John Cusack** and **Steven Spielberg**. Here we discuss the high price of being a celebrity with its loss of privacy and threats to one's life and family members. Without a doubt Stalkers are truly a **CELEBRITY CURSE**.

My next book delved into the subject of capital punishment. It was titled the *Death Penalty Designee.* Capital Punishment is considered the third hot button issue after Abortion and Gun Control that most people try to avoid discussing. Everyone has some type of emotional attachment either for or against the Death Penalty without truly understanding the purpose or operation of the Death Penalty. The book doesn't take sides but provides the reader with facts and figures to support their positions. The issues are viewed through the eyes of a person, The Death Penalty Designee, who had to make the ultimate decisions of some of the most notorious cases of all times. The book starts with the Tookie Williams case and continues on with the Richard Ramirez (Night Stalker) case followed by the Bitter and Norris case eventually discussing dozens of homicides that everyone has faded memories of.

Another book was the *Killings on Route 66.* Part of American history can be told by all who have come west on the old Route 66. This book starts at the very end of Route 66 which is the Santa Monic pier where a number of nefarious cases occurred. Next we travel a few blocks to one of the sites where 10 innocent peoples were slaughtered. We follow Route 66 as it traverses through West Hollywood where Dominick Dunn became inspired to be a celebrated True Crime writer. Further on we come across the most horrific and diabolical double murder of all times in Hollywood. Of course we touch upon Dr. Haing Ngor's Killing Fields this time of LA as we stop for a deadly Dodger's game. It's amazing that not all the carnage on Route 66 came from traffic accidents.

A similar book I wrote was the *Killers on Mulholland Drive.* Here I travel down the highway to the Homes of the Stars. I start out relating the sad case of Ennis Cosby who was the victim of a Robbery Gone Bad. Then we weave our way on top of this famous highway to the estate of Marlon Brando where murder raised its ugly head by his son shooting his half-sister's finance while he sat on the sofa watching TV. We can't ignore what happened in his neighbor's house that being Jack

Nicholson. That was where Roman Polanski seduced a 14 year old girl and ultimately he became America's most famous fugitive. We examine how this road is Hollywood's Lovers Lane and at times it leads to deadly consequences.

One of my most fascinating books was the *Old Lady Killers.* For so many years I have been inundated with homicide cases involving male suspects. There have been a few female murder cases, but they involved women who generally want to knock off their husbands for the life insurance benefits. It is so rare to see a grandmother type committing crime. However, when I had to work on the Sante Kimes case, I couldn't believe how elderly women could be so evil. Next I worked on the case against Helen Golay (76) and Olga Rutterschmidt (74) who made a living caring for the homeless just to run over them to collect the life insurance policies they took out on these men. This book will definitely change your opinion about sweet little old ladies who can be incredibly malicious and wicked.

One of my Celerity books was the *Killing in the Castle.* Most readers are familiar with Phil Spector, the music producer, who brought us the 'Wall of Sound' and who was accused of killing an actress in his castle/house. However, few people know the true story of how this case labeled the 'Battle of the Experts' resulted in a hung jury. This case illustrates what happens when the defendant has unlimited resource and can hire dozens of Defense attorneys to represent him.

This next book was personal in nature for me to write. *Killing of a Legend* involved the double murder case of Mike Thompson the famous auto racing legend and his wife was one of the longest Unsolved Mysteries. A fledgling energetic Sheriff's detective took a new look at this old case and followed up on some obscure facts that unlocked the key to this case. This is a book about two men with giant egos in which one couldn't accept defeat. They took their disagreement all the way to the U.S. Supreme Court.

Another book was the *Killers on the Way to Vegas.* This book tells the story of two mothers who traveled halfway around the world to find their missing sons. It involved a case that fell between the cracks because the mothers didn't know where their sons were when they went missing. This is a story of how strong two mothers' love can be .They wouldn't accept defeat and ended up on the doorstep of the FBI in Los Angeles. There agents stepped up to the plate to solve one of the most mysterious cases by using a cadaver dog to sniff out a grave in the desert on the way to Vegas.

The LA True Crime series all began with this book the *Killer at the Door.* It discusses one of those cases in which the DA's Office originally prosecuted the wrong suspect. This book shows how a prosecutor had to right a wrong in order to get the killer at the door. The case has so many twists and turns over a ten year period it took to solve. A long the way this book will introduce the reader to the celebrity world as well as some of the zaniest characters you could ever image.

Made in the USA
Monee, IL
08 November 2026

67946336R00184